Dedication

This book is dedicated to Bhagawan Sri Sathya Sai Baba, my guru and guide who has inspired me through this journey.

Dear Esteemed Readers,

I am delighted to present "SECURING THE CI/CD PIPELINE: Best Practices for DevSecOps," a groundbreaking exploration where innovation converges with security in the dynamic landscape of modern software development. In this literary masterpiece, I take you through the intricacies of the Continuous Integration and Continuous Deployment (CI/CD) pipeline, shedding light on vulnerabilities in an era where velocity and reliability are paramount.

Starting with a compelling overview, I emphasize the pivotal role of the CI/CD pipeline and address the escalating security concerns surrounding it. Together, we traverse the world of DevSecOps, seamlessly integrating security into your pipeline while harnessing cutting-edge Web3 technologies to fortify your development process.

As we progress through this insightful expedition, we embark on a quest to understand the core components of the CI/CD pipeline, illuminating phases and addressing concealed security challenges. DevSecOps principles become imperative, and I guide you through these principles to ensure the invulnerability of your software delivery.

This literary masterpiece stands out with its treasury of practical insights and avant-garde solutions. From automating compliance through Policy-as-Code (PaC) to securing containerized environments and fostering collaboration between development and security teams, you will discover knowledge to elevate your CI/CD pipeline.

Real-world case studies vividly illustrate the benefits of Infrastructure-as-Code (IaC) and PaC in the dynamic software development landscape. Meticulously crafted tables serve as guiding stars, illuminating the path toward a robust and efficient CI/CD pipeline.

As our epic voyage nears its conclusion, I underscore the paramount importance of pipeline security in the face of cyber threats, highlighting the indispensable role of DevSecOps in achieving unwavering security.

But that's not all. "Navigating the CI/CD Pipeline" takes you on a thrilling adventure through the intersection of innovation and security, providing pragmatic solutions for conquering challenges, integrating testing tools, harmonizing Web3 technologies, and more.

In a separate expedition, "A Comprehensive Guide to Harnessing DevSecOps CI/CD Pipeline Open-Source Project Monitoring, Self-Assessment, and Metric Management Tools," I invite you to explore open-source tools empowering organizations to balance speed and safety in the DevSecOps journey.

Among these tools, the "Policy as Code (PaC) Best Practice Assessment" stands out as a beacon of knowledge and automation, systematically elevating your organization's security posture.

This volume transcends the realm of books; it is your passport to a future where DevSecOps excellence becomes a way of life. Offering an exhilarating voyage through the CI/CD pipeline leads to swifter, safer software development and realizing your aspirations. To access the hands-on open-source tool and engage with me, please get in touch with devsecops999@gmail.com or stay connected through LinkedIn.

As you embark on this enlightening DevSecOps expedition, remember that security is not a supplement but an integral cornerstone of innovation. Armed with the wisdom contained herein, you are poised to champion secure software delivery and usher in a new era of digital excellence.

Sincerely,

Sai Sravan Cherukuri

Happy reading!

Introduction to My Open-Source CI/CD Monitoring Hands-on Tool

I am thrilled to introduce my groundbreaking open-source tool, designed to simplify the onboarding process for new or existing projects onto a Continuous Integration/Continuous Deployment (CI/CD) pipeline. This meticulously crafted resource offers a comprehensive checklist and a range of monitoring, measurement, and compliance-check tools aligned to meet regulatory requirements.

In today's ever-evolving technological landscape, adopting CI/CD practices is not just a choice but a necessity for organizations striving to strike the delicate balance between speed and security. My open-source tool, featured in this compendium, empowers organizations with the essential tools and knowledge for effective project monitoring, self-assessment, and proficient management of technical and project metrics.

The main objectives of this comprehensive guide are as follows:

1. **Onboarding Facilitation**: I have provided a step-by-step onboarding process that ensures a seamless transition of projects onto a CI/CD pipeline. This process is designed to minimize disruptions, increase efficiency, and enhance the overall productivity of project teams.

2. **Regulatory Compliance**: My tool equips organizations with compliance-check mechanisms in an environment where regulatory requirements continually evolve, ensuring that all projects adhere to the necessary regulations and standards.

3. **Project Monitoring**: My tool offers an array of gears to empower organizations to track project progress in real-time, allowing for proactive intervention when necessary and ensuring alignment with organizational goals.

4. **Measurement and Metrics Management**: Effective measurement and metrics management are at the core of a successful CI/CD pipeline. This guide provides insights into setting up and using these tools proficiently, enabling organizations to make informed decisions and drive continuous improvement.

I encourage you to contact me to obtain a copy of this hands-on open-source tool featured in this book. By doing so, you will take the first step towards harnessing the immense potential of CI/CD in your organization and achieving unparalleled project agility, security, and success.

If you have any questions, require additional information, or need assistance, please don't hesitate to contact me. I look forward to participating in your journey to mastering the art of CI/CD.

CI/CD Pipeline - Project Monitoring, Self Assessment, and Metric Management Tools

	Worksheet Title	Worksheet Objective
Project Monitoring Tool	DevSecOps Project Monitoring Tool	DevSecOps Project Monitoring Tools play a crucial role in modern software development by providing real-time insights into the security posture of applications throughout their lifecycle. These tools enable organizations to integrate security into their DevOps processes seamlessly.
Self Assessment Tools	Assessment of Security Challenges with DevSecOps	Assessing Security Challenges with DevSecOps involves identifying and mitigating the unique security risks and obstacles that arise when implementing DevSecOps practices. This assessment helps organizations understand how to balance speed and security effectively.
	Infrastructure as Code (IaC) Best Practices Assessment	Evaluating Infrastructure as Code (IaC) Best Practices involves examining how infrastructure is defined and provisioned using code, aiming to optimize efficiency, reliability, and security in modern cloud environments.
	Policy as Code (PaC)Best Practice Assessment	Policy as Code (PaC) Best Practice Assessment focuses on defining and enforcing security and compliance policies through code, ensuring that infrastructure and applications adhere to specified standards.
	Fortify and Flourish: Mastering Container Security and Self Assessment	Container security is a critical aspect of DevSecOps. This topic involves mastering container security practices and conducting self-assessments to ensure secure containerized applications.
	Technical Debt Assessment in the DevSecOps	Managing Technical Debt in DevSecOps involves evaluating and addressing the accumulated shortcuts, compromises, and suboptimal practices in software development to maintain a sustainable security posture.
	Zero Trust Maturity Model	The Zero Trust Maturity Model outlines a framework for organizations to adopt a Zero Trust security approach. This model progressively enhances security by reducing trust assumptions and continuously verifying trustworthiness.
	Federal Information Security Management Act (FISMA) Assessment	The FISMA Assessment focuses on evaluating and ensuring compliance with federal information security standards and regulations, which is particularly crucial for government agencies and organizations handling sensitive data.
	DevSecOps Maturity Model (DSOMM) Assessment	The DevSecOps Maturity Model (DSOMM) Assessment helps organizations gauge their maturity level in integrating security into the DevOps pipeline, guiding them towards continuous improvement.
	Open Source Security Knowledge Automation (OSKAR) Framework.	The OSKAR Framework is designed to automate the acquisition and application of open-source security knowledge, providing organizations with a systematic approach to enhancing their security posture.
Technical and Project Metric Management Tool	Metric Definitions	Metric Definitions involve clarifying the key performance indicators (KPIs) and metrics used to measure the effectiveness and efficiency of DevSecOps practices.
	Sample DevSecOps Technical Dashboard	A Sample DevSecOps Technical Dashboard visually represents essential security and operational metrics, helping teams monitor and manage their DevSecOps processes effectively.
	Data	Data is the foundation of any DevSecOps initiative. This topic may involve discussing data collection, storage, analysis, and visualization techniques critical for decision-making in DevSecOps practices.

CI/CD Pipeline-Project Onboarding Process

Introduction: This onboarding checklist outlines essential activities for onboarding application teams onto the DevSecOps capabilities. It is a foundation for customizing onboarding activities tailored to the Organization's needs. Clear ownership is assigned to relevant teams (e.g., Teams, Service Desk, Op-Prem or Cloud Technical Team) for each activity. This checklist ensures accountability and the completion of necessary onboarding tasks.

I. Initial Planning and Assessment	II. Pre-Onboarding Preparation
1. Define Objectives: Clearly outline the objectives and goals of the onboarding process.	**4. Infrastructure Setup:** Provision necessary infrastructure and resources for the new teams.
Owner: DevSecOps Onboarding Team	*Owner: Cloud Technical Team*
2. Identify Application Teams: Identify the application teams to be onboarded.	**5. Tooling Configuration:** Configure CI/CD tools and platforms as per project requirements.
Owner: Project Manager	*Owner: DevSecOps Engineer*
3. Assess Current Environment: Evaluate the existing development and deployment practices.	**6. Access and Permissions:** Grant appropriate access and permissions to tools and repositories.
Owner: DevOSecps Architect	*Owner: Security Team*

III. Training and Knowledge Transfer	IV. CI/CD Pipeline Setup
7. DevOps Training: Organize training sessions on DevOps principles and practices for application teams.	**9. Pipeline Design:** Design CI/CD pipelines tailored to each application's needs.
Owner: DevSecOps Trainer	*Owner: DevSecOps Engineer*
8. Documentation: Provide comprehensive documentation on CI/CD pipelines and processes.	**10. Integration Testing:** Set up automated integration testing in the pipeline.
Owner: Documentation Team	*Owner: Quality Assurance Team*
	11. Security Scanning: Integrate security scanning tools for vulnerability assessment.
	Owner: Security Team

V. Automation and Monitoring	VI. Deployment and Testing
12. Automation Rules: Define automation rules and triggers for deployments.	**14. Deployment Automation:** Implement automated deployment processes.
Owner: DevSecOps Engineer	*Owner: DevSecOps Engineer*
13. Monitoring and Alerting: Set up monitoring and alerting systems for the CI/CD pipelines.	**15. Staging Environment:** Create a staging environment for testing changes before production.
Owner: Operations Team	*Owner: Operations Team*

VII. Post-Onboarding Review	VIII. Ongoing Support and Collaboration
16. Performance Review: Conduct a post-onboarding review to assess the effectiveness of the onboarding process. -	**18. Support Channels:** Establish communication channels for ongoing support and collaboration between application teams and DevOps. -
Owner: DevOps Onboarding Team	*Owner: Service Desk*
17. Continuous Improvement: Identify areas for improvement and iterate on the onboarding process.	**19. Feedback Loop:** Encourage regular feedback from application teams to enhance the DevOps pipeline.
Owner: DevSecOps Champion	*Owner: DevSecOps Onboarding Team*

IX. Finalization and Handoff	
20. Completion Checklist: Ensure all onboarding activities are completed and validated.	**21. Handoff to Operations:** Transition ownership and support responsibility to the Operations Team.
Owner: DevSecOps Onboarding Team	*Owner: DevOps Onboarding Team*

Conclusion: This checklist is a comprehensive guide to facilitate the smooth onboarding of application teams into the DevSecOps ecosystem. It emphasizes clear responsibilities, well-defined tasks, and ongoing collaboration to enhance and automate the process. Successful onboarding is pivotal for optimizing software development within the Organization.

CI/CD Pipeline -Project Onboarding Checklist

1.Customize Onboarding Checklist: Alter the checklist to match your company's requirements.
2.Assign Activity Owners: Designate responsible teams (e.g., Teams, Service Desk, Cloud Technical Team) for each task.
3.Share Customized Checklist: Provide the customized checklist to the DevSecOps onboarding team for accountability.
4.Effective Onboarding Components: Recognize the logistical and strategic aspects involved in onboarding software development teams.
5.Common Pitfalls: Understand the challenges of this critical stage, such as unclear responsibilities and undefined tasks.
6.Use the Framework as a Guide: Employ this framework as a guideline to streamline and automate the onboarding process.
7.Focus on Software Development: Ensure that the team focuses on software development for a successful onboarding experience.

Product Information
What is the current project vision and mission?

Project Name		Vision	
Product Lead			
Product Duration			
Members		Users	

Delivery Methodology
What methodologies does the team use to deliver the software? ✔ the relevant boxes

| ✔ JIRA | ✗ Confluence Space | Kanban | Other 1 | Other 3 |
| TRELLO | Scrum | Extreme Programming | Other 2 | Other 4 |

Software Language & Development Frameworks
What languages and frameworks are the development team using to deliver the software? ✔ the relevant boxes

Software product and environment Details

Category	Options					Owner	Completion Date
Project Source Repository Exists	GIT	SVN	CVS	Other 1	Other 2 / Other 3		
Programming Language	Java Script	Python	Java	C++ / C	PHP / Swift		
	C#	Ruby	Objective-C	SQL	Other 3 / Other 1		
Developmental Platforms	Unknown	Linux	Windows	Android	AWS / MAC OS		
	iOS	Rasberry Pi	Firebase	Azure	Heroku / Arduino		
	Google Cloud	Serverless	SAP	Apple Watch or TV	IBM Cloud or Watson / Google Home		
	Gaming Console	Mainframe	Other 1	Other 2	Other 3 / Other 4		
	Web Dev	Mobile Dev	Data Science	App Dev	Back-end Dev / API Dev		
	Cloud Computing	Security Software Dev	Embedded Systems Dev	Other DEV	Other DEV / Other DEV		
Integrated Developer Environments	Atom	CLion	Cloud9	Code2	Code::Blocks / Codelresh		
	CodeLite	Eclipse	Eric Python IDE	Geany	Idle IDE / IntelliJ IDEA		
	JCreator	KDevelop	Komodo	Lazarus	Light Table / Microsoft Visual Studio IDE		
	Monkey Studio	MyEclipse	NetBeans IDE	Nuclide	Other / Squad		
	NuSphere PhpED	PhpStorm	PyCharm	Qt Creator	RubyMine / SapphireSteel		
	Visual LANSA	Visual Studio Code	WebStorm	Xamarin	Xcode / Zend Studio		

Assigning Project Roles

Does the requesting team meet all of the onboarding requirements?

Onboarding Requirements	Status	Tick / Cross	Issues (if any)	Completion Date
Project Name is Valid			Issues (if any)	
Project members are valid			Issues (if any)	
Valid software project			Issues (if any)	
Development Platform Supported			Issues (if any)	
Software Development type supported		Set Status	Issues (if any)	
IDE's Supported		Tick if Green	Issues (if any)	
Programming Language Supported		Cross if Not Green	Issues (if any)	
<Other ...>			Issues (if any)	
<Other ...>			Issues (if any)	
<Other ...>			Issues (if any)	
<Other ...>			Issues (if any)	
<Other ...>			Issues (if any)	

Supported DevOps pipeline

The software which is being written by the development team - Supported software product and environment details

Category	Options					Owner	Completion Date
Development Platforms	Linux	AWS	MAC OS	Serverless	Other 1 / Other 2		
Types of Software Development	Web Dev	App Dev	Cloud Computing	Back-end Dev	Other / Other		
Integrated Developer Environments	IntelliJ IDEA	Microsoft Visual Studio IDE	PhpStorm	PyCharm	Visual Studio Code / Other		
Programming languages	Python	Java / Scala	Go	Javascript	C++ / Other		
	Other	Other	Other	Other	Other / Other		

Table of Contents

List of Tables

I. Introduction

A. Overview of the CI/CD Pipeline and Its Importance in Software Development

In contemporary software development, the Continuous Integration/Continuous Deployment (CI/CD) pipeline is a linchpin, serving as a vital enabler for development teams. Its role in application building, testing, and deployment automation cannot be overstated, resulting in faster and more efficient software delivery. By breaking down the development process into discrete, manageable stages, the CI/CD pipeline paves the way for the frequent integration and deployment of code, thus fostering collaboration among developers and substantially curtailing time-to-market.

The CI/CD pipeline, an indispensable set of practices and tools within the domain of software development, has ushered in a new era of automation. Its core objective is to streamline and expedite the intricate processes associated with building, testing, and deploying software changes. Doing so empowers development teams to deliver code with greater clarity and reliability. By ensuring that software updates undergo rigorous testing and are deployed meticulously, the CI/CD pipeline instills confidence in the development process and minimizes the risk of unintended consequences.

The CI/CD pipeline emerges as an imperative catalyst in the relentless pursuit of software development excellence. Its ability to harmonize speed, reliability, and quality not only enhances the efficiency of development teams but also propels organizations into a more competitive and agile future.

Embrace the CI/CD pipeline, for it is a cornerstone in the edifice of modern software development, which promises to reshape how we create and deliver software in the digital age.

Continuous Integration (CI) stands as an unmistakable beacon of best practices. This section underscores the pivotal significance of CI while elucidating its essential components, interweaving fundamental principles that enhance code quality, collaboration, and risk mitigation.

1. **Continuous Integration (CI):**
Continuous Integration is the bedrock of agile software development, promoting the frequent merging of code changes from multiple developers into a central repository, often several times daily. The fundamental goal of CI is to promptly identify and resolve integration issues, ultimately reducing the risk of conflicts and elevating overall code quality. A sequence of meticulously structured steps characterizes this practice:

> **a. Code Repository:** Developers employ version control systems like Git to harmoniously commit code changes to a shared repository, fostering a unified and up-to-date codebase.

> **b. Automated Build:** The CI server automatically retrieves the latest code from the repository, compiling and constructing the software consistently and reliably. This step guarantees that the software remains in a perpetually deployable state.

> **c. Automated Tests:** A comprehensive suite of automated tests rigorously scrutinizes the code's integrity, adhering to predefined quality standards and mitigating the risk of defects. This diligent testing regimen is the hallmark of robust software development.

> **d. Reporting:** Test results, code coverage metrics, and other salient data are meticulously generated, offering valuable insights into the codebase's quality and adherence to established criteria. These insights guide data-driven decision-making.

> **e. Notification:** Prompt communication embodies the spirit of CI. Developers are expediently alerted to build or test failures, arming them with the necessary information to rectify issues. This enhances team collaboration and maintains the project's trajectory and quality.

Continuous Integration (CI)

1.Code Repository:
Developers use a version control system (such as Git) to commit their changes to a shared repository.

2.Automated Build:
The CI server automatically pulls the latest code from the repository, compiles it, and builds the software.

3. Automated Tests:
A suite of automated tests is executed to validate the integrity of the code and ensure that it meets quality standards.

4. Reporting:
Test results, code coverage metrics, and other relevant information are generated, providing insights into the quality of the codebase.

5. Notification:
Developers are notified of any build or test failures, allowing them to fix issues promptly.

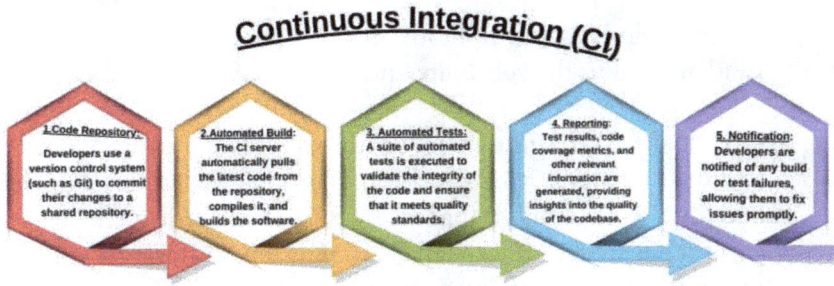

The profound impact of Continuous Integration (CI) cannot be understated. CI cultivates an environment where issues are identified and resolved early, reducing the risk of conflicts and improving overall code quality. Collaboration among team members flourishes in this iterative and communicative atmosphere as developers work harmoniously towards a common goal. Within the crucible of CI, software development thrives, underpinning the principles of excellence and efficiency that drive our industry forward.

2. Continuous Deployment (CD):

The practice of Continuous Deployment (CD) stands as a critical enabler for teams aiming to automate the release and Deployment of software changes to production environments. This section meticulously outlines the essential components of CD, shedding light on the pivotal steps that facilitate frequent and dependable software releases while underscoring its vital role in the development process.

Continuous Deployment epitomizes the essence of automated software release and Deployment to production environments, unlocking the potential for recurrent and reliable software releases. The CD comprises a series of meticulously orchestrated steps, each pivotal to its overall success:

  a. Automated Deployment: Following successful integration and rigorous CI/CD pipeline testing, the CD process automatizes Software Deployment to staging or production environments. This seamless transition ensures that the software is made accessible to end-users swiftly and consistently.

  b. Environment Configuration: The deployment process is central in ensuring the target environment is accurately

3

configured, incorporating all essential dependencies and configurations. A harmonious and well-prepared environment is fundamental to the reliability and success of each Deployment.

c. Release Management: CD orchestrates the management of software versions with precision. Through versioning, tagging, and the meticulous management of release notes, teams can comprehensively track and administer different software versions, thus empowering effective version control and transparency.

d. Monitoring and Rollbacks: Continuous monitoring of the deployed application is fundamental in real-time issue detection. If issues arise, the CD pipeline is fortified with automated rollback mechanisms that can revert to the previous version, minimizing disruptions. These mechanisms reduce manual errors, ensuring an accelerated time-to-market and the ability to promptly deliver new features and bug fixes to end-users.

The significance of Continuous Deployment cannot be understated. CD operates as an engine of precision and efficiency, allowing teams to expedite software releases, minimize manual errors, and uphold a seamless and consistent software delivery process. In doing so, it equips development teams with the capability to swiftly deliver new features and address issues while fostering a reliable and robust software deployment environment.

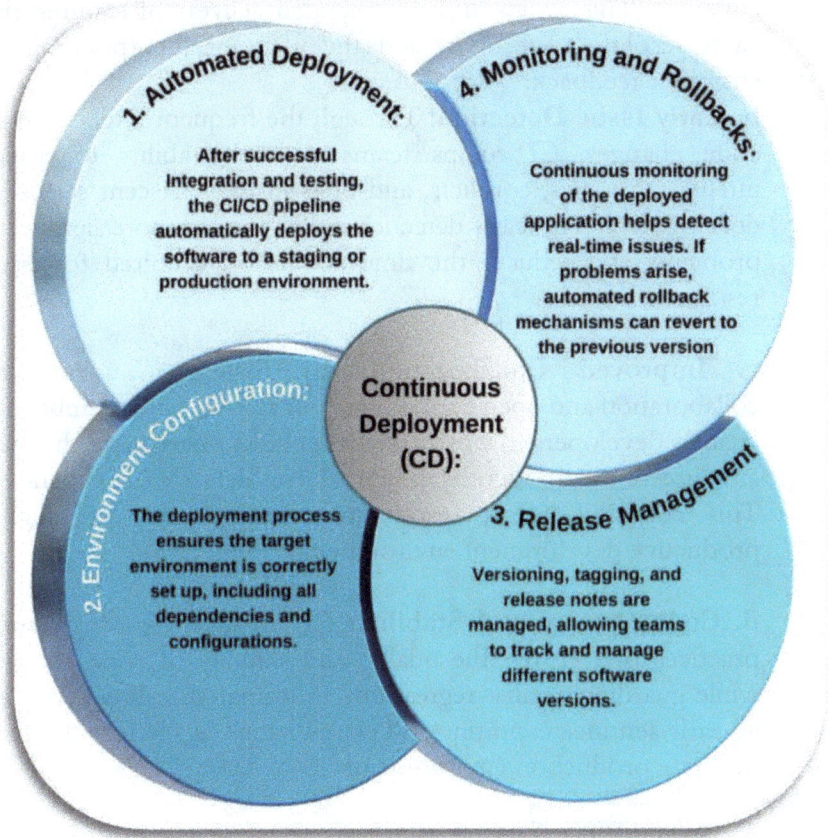

1. Automated Deployment:
After successful Integration and testing, the CI/CD pipeline automatically deploys the software to a staging or production environment.

4. Monitoring and Rollbacks:
Continuous monitoring of the deployed application helps detect real-time issues. If problems arise, automated rollback mechanisms can revert to the previous version

Continuous Deployment (CD):

2. Environment Configuration:
The deployment process ensures the target environment is correctly set up, including all dependencies and configurations.

3. Release Management
Versioning, tagging, and release notes are managed, allowing teams to track and manage different software versions.

3. **Importance of CI/CD in Software Development:**

Adopting Continuous Integration/Continuous Deployment (CI/CD) pipelines is transformative. This section emphasizes the pivotal importance of CI/CD in the software development process, articulating its multifaceted benefits and its primary role in elevating the standards of modern software delivery.

Continuous Integration and Continuous Deployment (CI/CD) pipelines usher in a host of substantial benefits that resonate throughout the software development lifecycle:

    a. **Faster Time-to-Market:** Automated build, test, and deployment processes furnish development teams with the capability to release software changes with remarkable speed and reliability. This results in the accelerated delivery of features, the swift resolution of bugs, and the efficient incorporation of customer feedback.

b. Early Issue Detection: Through the frequent integration of code changes, CI equips teams with the ability to detect integration issues, conflicts, and bugs in their nascent stages of development. This early detection helps prevent more significant problems and reduces the time and effort required for issue resolution.

c. Improved Collaboration: CI fosters a culture of collaboration and open communication among team members. It enables developers to work on parallel tasks, share code changes, and preemptively identify potential conflicts or dependencies. This collective effort results in a harmonious and highly productive development environment.

d. Code Quality and Stability: CI enforces rigorous testing practices that ensure the quality and stability of code changes while guarding against regressions. Automated testing serves as an early sentinel, capturing and neutralizing bugs before they can infiltrate production environments.

e. Scalability and Reliability: Continuous Deployment automates the deployment process, ensuring consistency across diverse environments. This reduction in human error safeguards the reliability of deployments and empowers the efficient scaling of operations.

f. Continuous Feedback Loop: CI/CD pipelines are designed to generate comprehensive reports, metrics, and test results, thereby furnishing teams with a continuous feedback loop on the health and quality of the software. This invaluable feedback is the bedrock for data-driven decisions, enabling the refinement and enhancement of development processes.

The CI/CD pipeline is an asset and a cornerstone of modern software development practices. It ushers in an era of automation in build, testing, and deployment, which translates into faster releases, elevated code quality, and fortified collaboration. With CI/CD, development teams have the power to deliver software with unmatched efficiency, reliability, and a considerably reduced time-to-market. The adoption of CI/CD is not merely a choice; it is a strategic imperative.

Imagine a scenario in which a software development team working on a complex web application is empty of a CI/CD pipeline. In this scenario, each code change necessitates manual testing and deployment, a time-consuming process and susceptible to errors. However, with a robust CI/CD pipeline, developers orchestrate these processes with automated precision, assuring that changes are thoroughly tested, seamlessly integrated, and consistently deployed. The result is software marked by heightened reliability and stability, a testament to the transformative power of CI/CD.

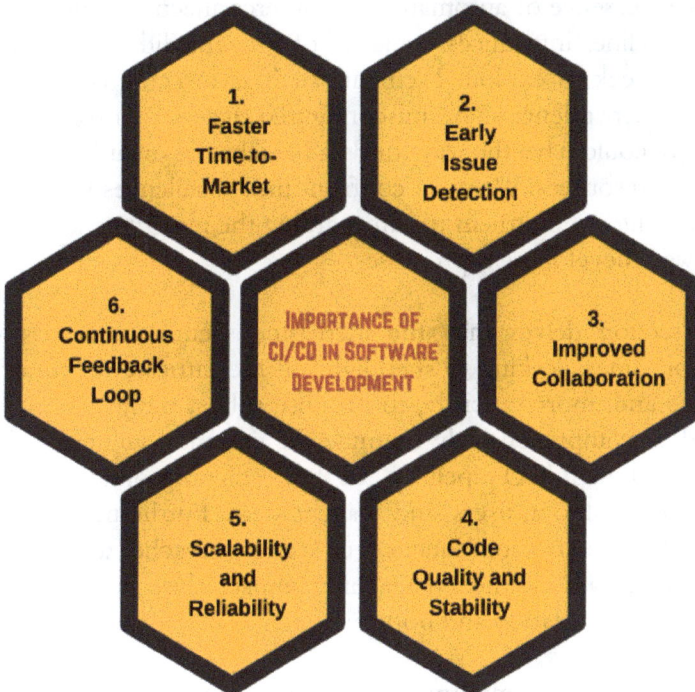

B. Growing Security Concerns in CI/CD Pipelines

In the ever-evolving software development landscape, the advent of Continuous Integration/Continuous Deployment (CI/CD) pipelines has ushered in a transformative era. These pipelines have become pivotal in automating application building, testing, and deployment, revolutionizing the industry by significantly expediting software delivery. However, distinct and escalating security concerns loom amidst the remarkable advantages of CI/CD pipelines, demanding a comprehensive and authoritative response.

The very essence of automation and interconnectivity, integral to the CI/CD pipeline, introduces an array of vulnerabilities that malicious actors may seek to exploit. Elements such as insecure configurations, unpatched dependencies, or misconfigured access controls, once left unchecked, could pave the way for data breaches or unauthorized access to sensitive resources. We must confront these challenges head-on, with an unwavering commitment to safeguarding the integrity and security of our software development processes.

This section delves into the increasing security concerns within CI/CD pipelines, seeking to shed light on the intricate nature of these challenges and, more crucially, to propose robust mitigation strategies. We need to comprehensively examine the common vulnerabilities and risks inherent in CI/CD pipelines, for they can compromise our projects and the trust of our users and stakeholders. Furthermore, we must confront the potential consequences of security breaches with the utmost seriousness, aware of the far-reaching impact they can have on our organization's reputation and bottom line.

In our unceasing commitment to excellence, I present a collection of best practices to enhance the security of our CI/CD pipelines. When meticulously implemented, these practices safeguard against the ever-evolving threat landscape and are a testament to our dedication to delivering efficient and impervious software to security vulnerabilities.

Common Security Concerns:

The following section serves as an authoritative exploration of these concerns, underlining their gravity and proposing strategies to safeguard the integrity of our pipelines.

1. Inadequate Access Controls: Weak access controls within CI/CD pipelines constitute a formidable vulnerability. They can permit unauthorized access, the manipulation of source code, and the accidental exposure of sensitive information. Inadequately managed access rights expose us to the risk of malicious actors compromising the pipeline and introducing nefarious code into our deployment process.

2. Vulnerability in External Dependencies: CI/CD pipelines often depend on third-party libraries and dependencies. However, these dependencies may harbor known vulnerabilities or become tampered with, creating an entry point for security threats. Neglecting these dependencies' regular updating and monitoring can leave our pipelines susceptible to potential attacks.

3. Insecure Configuration Management: Misconfigurations in CI/CD pipeline tools and platforms represent another significant concern. These misconfigurations may result in unintended security gaps, such as insecurely stored credentials, improper permission settings, or the exposure of unencrypted sensitive data. These issues can lead to unauthorized access or data leakage.

4. Code Injection and Malware Attacks: CI/CD pipelines that lack proper input validation or fail to employ security scanning tools are susceptible to code injection attacks. Malicious actors can exploit these vulnerabilities to inject malicious code or malware into the pipeline, compromising the integrity of the entire software release process.

5. Insider Threats: Even insiders with authorized access to CI/CD pipelines pose a unique security challenge. These threats can range from accidental misconfigurations to intentional sabotage or data theft. Thus, safeguarding against insider threats necessitates a multifaceted approach.

These security concerns should call for unwavering vigilance and proactive measures. Our collective responsibility is to ensure that our

CI/CD pipelines remain resilient in the face of these challenges, safeguarding the integrity of our software releases and, by extension, the trust of our stakeholders.

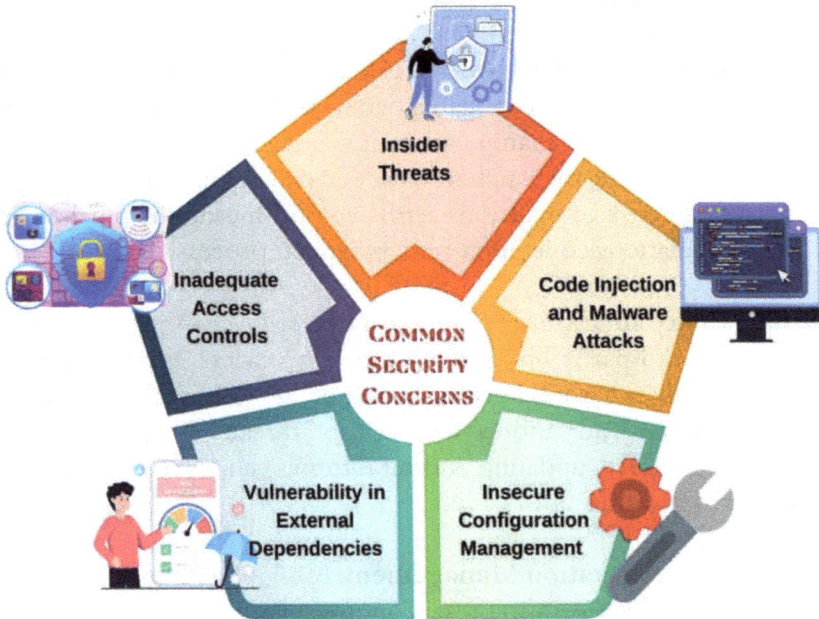

Safeguarding Software Integrity and Reputation in CI/CD Pipelines:

The transformative practices of CI/CD pipelines bring unprecedented security concerns that demand our unwavering attention and immediate action. These concerns underscore the need for robust security measures to preserve software integrity and safeguard the organization's reputation.

1. Compromised Software Integrity:

Security breaches within CI/CD pipelines can lead to a dire compromise of software integrity. Such breaches may culminate in deploying compromised software to production environments, thus setting the stage for potential data breaches, service disruptions, and unauthorized access to sensitive information. The implications of such breaches are far-reaching, impacting both the organization and its stakeholders.

2. Reputation and Financial Losses:

A security incident can inflict severe harm upon an organization's reputation and erode the trust of its customers. Beyond reputational damage, the costs associated with incident response, remediation, and potential legal liabilities can be financially substantial. These repercussions highlight the critical importance of proactive security measures.

As CI/CD pipelines become increasingly ubiquitous in the realm of software development, it is incumbent upon organizations to confront and rectify their burgeoning security challenges. By rigorously implementing and adhering to robust security practices, organizations can effectively mitigate risks, ensuring the integrity of software and the protection of sensitive data throughout the software release process. The key to this security framework lies in continuous monitoring, regular updates, and security-focused education, all of which play pivotal roles in preserving the security and reliability of CI/CD pipelines.

A stark illustration of the severity of these concerns surfaced in the Codecov attack of April 2021. In this incident, hackers illicitly accessed Codecov's Bash Uploader, an integral CI/CD process tool, and clandestinely inserted a malicious script. This breach enabled them to harvest sensitive credentials and infiltrate various organizations' code repositories, jeopardizing their source code and sensitive information.

In the ever-dynamic landscape of software development, security is not a mere facet of concern; it is a fundamental imperative. The preservation of software integrity, protection of sensitive data, and safeguarding of organizational reputation hinge on the proactive, unwavering commitment to robust security measures within CI/CD pipelines.

See chapter IV on Best Practices for Securing CI/CD Pipelines:

Table 1 **Fortifying DevSecOps:** Overcoming Security Challenges with Cutting-Edge Solutions

CI/CD Pipeline Phase	Security Challenges	Security Measures	Example of Real-world Implementation
Version Control and Source Code Management	Insecure storage of credentials, inadequate access controls, exposure of sensitive information through improperly managed repositories	Implement secure credential management practices. Enforce strong access controls. Employ secure repository management practices.	Example: GitHub, one of the popular version control platforms, provides organizations with features to address these security challenges. They offer encrypted storage for sensitive information like API keys and passwords using GitHub Secrets. Access controls can be enforced through granular permissions and two-factor authentication (2FA). Additionally, organizations can use GitHub's vulnerability scanning and dependency management tools to detect vulnerabilities in code and dependencies.
Continuous Integration	Code injection, insecure dependencies, lack of secure coding practices	Implement automated security testing (SAST). Regularly scan and update dependencies. Educate developers on secure coding practices.	For example, Jenkins, a widely used CI/CD tool, allows the integration of security plugins like OWASP Dependency-Check and SonarQube for automated security testing. These plugins scan code for vulnerabilities and provide reports to developers. Organizations can also use tools like Nexus Repository Manager to manage and update dependencies securely. Organizations can proactively address security challenges by integrating these tools into the CI/CD pipeline.

Continuous Deployment	Mis-configurations, Unauthorized deployments, Insecure container images	Establish secure deployment configuration management practices Implement strict access controls Utilize container image scanning tools	Example: Kubernetes, an open-source container orchestration platform, offers various features to address deployment security challenges. Organizations can define and enforce security policies using Kubernetes' Role-Based Access Control (RBAC) to prevent unauthorized deployments. Configuration management tools like Helm enable organizations to manage and deploy applications securely with version control and rollback capabilities. Additionally, container image scanning tools like Anchore and Aqua Security can be integrated to scan container images for vulnerabilities before deployment.
Code Development	Lack of secure coding practices and vulnerability detection	Code reviews, static code analysis tools, and secure coding guidelines	Implementing code review process using automated static code analysis tools such as SonarQube. Conducting regular training sessions on secure coding practices.
Continuous Integration	Insecure third-party dependencies and integration vulnerabilities	Regular vulnerability scanning and dependency management	Integration of dependency scanning tools like OWASP Dependency-Check into the CI process to identify and address vulnerabilities in third-party libraries. Implementation of a robust vulnerability management program.
Build and Packaging	Inadequate security controls for build artifacts and misconfiguration	Automated build artifact signing, secure configuration management, and vulnerability scanning	Implement secure signing and verification processes using tools like GPG (GNU Privacy Guard) to build artifacts. Utilizing tools like Docker Content Trust to ensure the integrity of container images. Regular vulnerability scanning of build artifacts using tools like Anchore.

Deployment and Orchestration	Weak access controls, insecure configurations, and mismanaged secrets	Role-based access controls, secure configuration management, and secrets management	Utilizing tools like Kubernetes RBAC (Role-Based Access Control) infrastructure-as-code (IaC) with secure configuration templates. Employing secrets management tools like HashiCorp Vault to store and distribute sensitive information securely.
Infrastructure Monitoring	Lack of visibility into security events, inadequate logging, and monitoring	Security event logging, centralized log management, and security monitoring tools	Execution of a SIEM (Security Information and Event Management) solution to collect and analyze security events. Centralized log aggregation using ELK (Elasticsearch, Logstash, Kibana) and employing intrusion detection and prevention systems (IDPS) for real-time monitoring and alerting.
Testing and Quality Assurance	Insufficient security testing, inadequate test coverage, and lack of secure test data	Security testing frameworks, code review in test cases, and secure test data management	Integrating security testing tools like OWASP ZAP and Burp Suite into the testing process. Conducting code reviews of test cases to identify potential security vulnerabilities. Using secure test data generation techniques to ensure the confidentiality of sensitive data.
Release and Deployment	Unauthorized release, misconfigured deployment, and lack of rollback plan	Release management processes, deployment automation, and rollback strategies	Implementing a well-defined release management process with appropriate approval workflows. Utilizing deployment automation tools like Jenkins or GitLab CI/CD pipelines. Establishing rollback strategies and conducting release validation tests before production deployment.
Incident Response	Lack of incident response plan, inefficient communication channels, and inadequate forensic capabilities	Incident response planning, communication protocols, and forensics tools	Developing an incident response plan with predefined roles and responsibilities. Establishing clear communication channels and escalation procedures. Utilizing forensics tools like OSSEC or Splunk for investigating security incidents. Regularly conducting incident response drills and tabletop exercises.

C. Introduction to DevSecOps and Its Role in Enhancing Pipeline Security

In the quest to counter the ever-mounting security challenges intrinsic to CI/CD pipelines, organizations increasingly turn to DevSecOps practices as the cornerstone of their defense. DevSecOps, an extension of the renowned DevOps paradigm, takes center stage by placing security at the forefront of the entire software development lifecycle. This transformative approach entails integrating security from the project's inception and continuously sustaining it throughout development. In doing so, DevSecOps aspires to cultivate a culture of cooperation and shared responsibility among development, security, and operations teams. This section delineates the tenets of DevSecOps and underscores its indispensable role in elevating the security of CI/CD pipelines.

Deciphering DevSecOps:

DevSecOps, the amalgamation of "Development," "Security," and "Operations," is driven by a fundamental objective—infusing security at every juncture of the software development lifecycle (SDLC). In contrast to conventional methodologies, where security is often relegated to a post-development phase, DevSecOps endorses a philosophy of seamlessly integrating security practices and tools into the very fabric of the development pipeline. Under this paradigm, security is a shared responsibility vested in all stakeholders, transcending the confines of siloed roles, and fostering a holistic approach to safeguarding software assets.

DevSecOps is no mere auxiliary endeavor; it is a strategic imperative. By eradicating the separation between security and development, organizations fortify their CI/CD pipelines and ensure that security is woven into the very DNA of their software projects. The result is an ecosystem where security is not a checkpoint but an integral part of the process. In this environment, software is developed quickly and efficiently and safeguarded with unwavering vigilance.

Critical Principles of DevSecOps: (also included in section III A)

1. **Shift-Left Approach:** DevSecOps encourages addressing security early in the SDLC, starting from the design and development stages,

rather than waiting until deployment or post-production. The cost and impact of potential security breaches can be significantly reduced by catching vulnerabilities and issues early.

2. **Automation and Continuous Monitoring**: Automation plays a crucial role in DevSecOps by enabling continuous security testing, code analysis, and monitoring throughout the pipeline. Automated security checks ensure that vulnerabilities are identified, analyzed, and addressed promptly, minimizing the time between bug detection and resolution.

3. **Collaboration and Communication:** DevSecOps fosters strong collaboration between development, operations, and security teams. Regular communication and shared responsibility enable a better understanding of security requirements, identify potential risks, and implement appropriate controls throughout the development lifecycle.

Role of DevSecOps in Enhancing Pipeline Security:

1. **Early Vulnerability Detection:** DevSecOps integrates automated security testing tools that continuously scan code repositories for potential vulnerabilities. Organizations can minimize the risk of deploying software with known vulnerabilities by identifying and addressing security flaws early in development.

2. **Security as Code**: By treating security configurations, policies, and controls as code, DevSecOps ensures consistency and repeatability. Security measures become part of the infrastructure-as-code (IaC) and can be managed, versioned, and audited alongside the application code. This approach facilitates the rapid provisioning of secure infrastructure and reduces the chances of misconfigurations and security gaps.

3. **Continuous Compliance:** DevSecOps enables organizations to maintain regulatory compliance throughout the SDLC. By automating compliance checks and integrating security controls into the pipeline, organizations can ensure adherence to industry

standards, regulations, and best practices, reducing the risk of non-compliance penalties.

4. **Threat Modeling and Risk Assessment:** DevSecOps encourages proactive identification and mitigation of potential threats. By conducting threat modeling exercises and risk assessments early on, development teams can anticipate and address security concerns before they escalate, strengthening the overall security posture.

5. **Incident Response and Recovery:** DevSecOps emphasizes the importance of robust incident response and recovery plans. By integrating security incident management processes into the development pipeline, organizations can minimize downtime, mitigate potential damage, and accelerate the resolution of security incidents.

DevSecOps, a harmonious amalgamation of security practices with the agile methodologies of DevOps, endorses a comprehensive strategy for developing and deploying software. By ingraining security principles across the entire development pipeline and fostering a culture of collaboration, organizations stand poised to elevate the integrity of their pipelines, decrease vulnerabilities, and respond decisively to emerging threats. The meticulous implementation of DevSecOps paves the way for teams to furnish secure software with swiftness, reinforcing customer trust and safeguarding invaluable digital assets amidst the complexities of the contemporary threat landscape.

An Exemplar in DevSecOps: Netflix

A global streaming giant, Netflix is an exemplary archetype of successful DevSecOps integration. The organization has wholeheartedly embraced the DevSecOps ethos, ensuring the security of its massive infrastructure and multifaceted applications. At the core of Netflix's approach is an adept synergy of automation, robust security tooling, and a seamless communication exchange among cross-functional teams. This harmonious blend allows them to proactively identify and address security vulnerabilities within their CI/CD pipeline. Netflix's proactive security measures illustrate how a robust DevSecOps framework enhances pipeline security and harmonizes with development velocity. In doing so, Netflix attains a secure, reliable, and swift software delivery process.

In the dynamic landscape of CI/CD pipelines, DevSecOps stands as a strategic imperative, a beacon illuminating the path towards attaining fortified security while simultaneously upholding the efficiency and agility that are the hallmarks of modern software development.

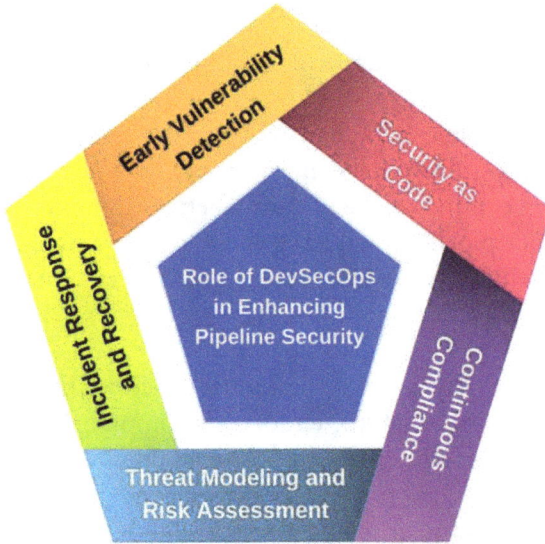

Table 2 **Strengthening Security:** Integrating Testing Tools into the Pipeline

Tools and Technologies	Description	Popular Tools
Static Application Security Testing (SAST):	SAST tools analyze source code, bytecode, or binary code to identify potential security vulnerabilities and coding errors. They perform a static analysis of the application's codebase, providing insights into common security issues like insecure coding practices, injection attacks, and configurations.	SonarQube, Checkmarx, and Fortify.
Dynamic Application Security Testing (DAST):	DAST tools evaluate web application security by simulating real-world attacks. These tools scan web applications for vulnerabilities like cross-site scripting (XSS), SQL injection, and insecure direct object references. They help identify vulnerabilities that may arise due to runtime behaviors or configurations.	OWASP ZAP, Burp Suite, and Netsparker.

Interactive Application Security Testing (IAST):	IAST tools combine aspects of both SAST and DAST approaches. They analyze the application during runtime and provide feedback on security vulnerabilities, offering real-time insights into code execution and application behavior. IAST tools can provide highly accurate results with reduced false positives.	Contrast Security, Seeker, and WhiteHat Security.
Software Composition Analysis (SCA):	SCA tools focus on identifying security vulnerabilities and open-source components with known vulnerabilities within an application's software supply chain. These tools scan application dependencies, libraries, and frameworks to highlight vulnerabilities and provide actionable recommendations for remediation.	Black Duck, Snyk, and Nexus Lifecycle.
Container Security:	Container security tools address security challenges specific to containerized environments. They focus on vulnerability scanning, image integrity, runtime protection, and secure orchestration of containers. These tools help ensure that containers are secure, compliant, and free from vulnerabilities.	Anchore, Sysdig Secure, and Aqua Security.
Infrastructure as Code (IaC) Security:	IaC security tools assess the security of infrastructure provisioning and deployment scripts, such as those written in tools like Terraform, CloudFormation, or Ansible. They scan IaC templates and configurations for security misconfigurations, insecure permissions, and potential vulnerabilities.	Checkov, Bridgecrew, and Prowler.
Security Orchestration, Automation, and Response (SOAR):	SOAR platforms enable organizations to streamline and automate security incident response processes. They integrate with various security tools, aggregate alerts, and orchestrate automated responses to security incidents. SOAR platforms help reduce response times, improve efficiency, and ensure consistent incident management practices.	Demisto (Palo Alto Networks), Splunk Phantom, and IBM Resilient.
Security Information and Event Management (SIEM):	SIEM tools collect, aggregate, and analyze security event logs from various sources within an IT infrastructure. They provide real-time threat detection, incident response, and compliance reporting capabilities. SIEM platforms are crucial in monitoring and correlating security events to identify potential threats.	Splunk Enterprise Security, IBM QRadar, and Elastic SIEM.

Security Testing Automation:	Security testing automation tools encompass various tools and frameworks for automating security testing activities. These tools include frameworks for security unit testing, vulnerability scanning, fuzz testing, and security test automation.	OWASP Security Shepherd, OWASP WebGoat, and Gauntlt.
Continuous Integration / Continuous Delivery (CI/CD) Security:	CI/CD security tools focus on integrating security practices into the CI/CD pipeline. They enable automated security checks, policy enforcement, and vulnerability scanning at each pipeline stage. CI/CD security tools help ensure that only secure and compliant code is deployed to production.	GitLab CI/CD, Jenkins, and CircleCI, with security plugins and integrations.

D. Empowering DevSecOps: Unveiling the Potential of Web3 for Secure and Agile Development

In software development, the perennial challenge has been to strike a harmonious balance between speed, quality, and security. However, the emergence of Web3 technology introduces a paradigm shift that holds the potential to revolutionize the DevSecOps ecosystem. Embracing the prospects of Web3 within DevSecOps signifies a profound departure towards secure, transparent, and collaborative development practices. Organizations can bolster their security stance by harnessing decentralization, smart contracts, and interoperability and cultivate an environment characterized by perpetual innovation. In this ever-evolving landscape, the watchwords are adaptability, proactivity, and vigilance.

The Web3 Advantage:
Web3 ushers in a transformative wave of advantages that eclipses the existing Web 2.0 architecture. At its core, decentralization redistributes authority from centralized entities to individuals, enhancing control over data and digital security. User empowerment takes center stage, granting ownership of data, identities, and assets, thus fostering active participation and informed consent. Its robust resistance to censorship is a standout feature, creating fertile ground for content and applications to flourish without fear of suppression. Interoperability is seamlessly

attained through protocols that bridge platforms, dismantling data silos and promoting fluidity.

In this expanding environment, the spirit of innovation thrives as Web3 incubates decentralized app creation, eliminating gatekeepers and nurturing an environment conducive to creativity. Trust finds a sturdy foundation in the transparency of blockchain and intelligent contracts, obviating the need for intermediaries and elevating accountability. Cryptocurrencies and blockchain drive financial inclusion, affording underserved communities access to the digital economy. The removal of intermediaries streamlines transactions, rendering them efficient and cost-effective.

Notably, Web3 champions data privacy through decentralized identity systems, extending control to users and curtailing data breaches. Its robustness against cyberattacks and single points of failure solidifies the resilience of decentralized networks. Yet, as the evolution of Web3 unfolds, it becomes imperative to acknowledge its trajectory and address its technical challenges. Furthermore, the coexistence of Web3 and Web 2.0 elements heralds the dawn of a hybrid digital landscape, amalgamating the strengths of both paradigms.

Integrating Web3 into DevSecOps epitomizes the evolution of secure, transparent, and collaborative development practices, offering unprecedented opportunities for innovation while upholding data integrity, security, and user empowerment.

Elevating DevSecOps: Unveiling the Intrinsic Value in this Ecosystem Enhancement.

Web3 concepts can bring several benefits to the DevSecOps (Development, Security, and Operations) ecosystem:

1. **Enhanced Security:** Web3's decentralized nature can reduce single points of failure and vulnerabilities. Smart contracts and cryptographic techniques can improve security in code deployment, authentication, and authorization processes.

2. **Immutable Audit Trails:** Blockchain's immutability can provide tamper-proof audit trails, helping to track changes in code, configurations, and security measures throughout the development lifecycle.

3. **Secure Identity and Access Management:** Decentralized identity systems can improve user authentication and access management and reduce the risk of unlawful access or data breaches.

4. **Automated Compliance:** Smart contracts can facilitate automatic compliance checks, ensuring code adheres to security standards and regulations before deployment.

5. **Trustless Collaboration:** Web3's intelligent contracts can establish trustless collaborations between different teams and stakeholders, automating agreements and ensuring security measures are upheld.

6. **Decentralized Application Security:** Developers can create dApps with security measures embedded in the protocol layer, reducing reliance on external security tools and attack surfaces.

7. **Tokenized Incentives:** Web3's tokenization can incentivize secure development practices by rewarding developers for identifying and fixing vulnerabilities.

8. **Decentralized Vulnerability Management:** Web3 technologies can enable the creation of decentralized vulnerability databases and disclosure platforms, allowing for more transparent reporting and fixing of security issues.

9. **Resilience to Attacks:** Decentralized networks are more resilient to certain types of cyberattacks, making it harder for malicious actors to disrupt services.

10. **Continuous Monitoring:** Blockchain's transparency and immutability can aid in continuously monitoring security events and breaches, ensuring rapid response and recovery.

11. **Secure Decentralized Infrastructure:** Web3 infrastructure, based on decentralized networks, can provide a more secure foundation for

applications and services, minimizing the risk of traditional infrastructure attacks.

For more information, refer to Table 3 and Table 4 **Navigating the Cutting Edge:** Unveiling the Web3 and DevSecOps Synergy with Tools of Tomorrow.

Navigating the Web3 Integration in DevSecOps

The prospects of integrating Web3 technologies into the DevSecOps paradigm are indeed promising, but it is paramount to tread this path with circumspection. As organizations venture into the world of Web3, they must reckon with a multifaceted landscape replete with learning curves, potential challenges, and inherent complexities accompanying these emerging technologies. Effectively harnessing the advantages of Web3 within the DevSecOps ecosystem necessitates meticulous planning, a commitment to education, and a willingness to adapt processes.

Embracing a Learning Curve:

Web3 technologies introduce a substantial learning curve, given their novelty and the radical shift they embody. DevSecOps teams and practitioners must invest in acquiring a deep understanding of these technologies to harness their potential effectively. This necessitates technical proficiency and an awareness of the unique paradigms and principles underpinning Web3.

Navigating Potential Challenges:

The adoption of Web3 technologies comes with its own set of challenges. These may include interoperability issues, the development of decentralized applications, the management of smart contracts, and the intricacies of blockchain technology. Organizations must be prepared to confront these challenges head-on, seeking solutions that align with their goals and security requirements.

Adapting to Complexity:

The complexity of Web3 technologies demands an adaptable mindset. Organizations must be willing to reshape their processes and workflows to accommodate the decentralized and interconnected nature of Web3. This may involve reevaluating security protocols, identity management, and data governance.

Meticulous Planning and Education:

Careful planning is a prerequisite for a successful integration of Web3 into DevSecOps. Organizations must define clear objectives, establish a roadmap, and allocate training and skill development resources. Education for technical staff and leadership is instrumental in ensuring a smooth transition.

In the face of these challenges and complexities, the commitment to continuous learning, strategic planning, and proactive adaptation will pave the way for a seamless integration of Web3 technologies into the DevSecOps ecosystem. While the journey may be arduous, the potential for enhanced security, transparency, and innovation that Web3 offers makes it worthwhile.

Table 3 **Harmonizing Innovation and Security:** Seamlessly Fusing Web3 Technologies into DevSecOps

Efficiently weaving Web3 technologies into the DevSecOps process demands a deliberate strategy and the skillful application of established methodologies. Presented here is a concise yet comprehensive guide.

1.	**Education and Training:**	• Ensure your DevSecOps team understands the fundamentals of blockchain, smart contracts, decentralized identity, and related Web3 concepts. • Provide training on the security implications and best practices associated with Web3 technologies.
2.	**Adapt Development Practices:**	• Incorporate the principles of decentralized application development into your coding practices. • Learn about innovative contract development and the programming languages commonly used in blockchain environments.
3.	**Decentralized Identity:**	• Explore decentralized identity solutions that enhance user authentication and access management. • Implement protocols like DID (Decentralized Identifier) and Verifiable Credentials for secure identity management.
4.	**Smart Contracts Security:**	• Learn about common vulnerabilities in smart contracts, such as reentrancy, integer overflow, and access control issues. • Use security tools and frameworks tailored to auditing intelligent contracts for vulnerabilities.
5.	**Continuous Integration and Deployment:**	• Integrate tools to analyze intelligent contract code for security issues as part of your CI/CD pipeline. • Set up automated tests and security checks for traditional code and smart contracts.
6.	**Immutable Audit Trails:**	• Explore how blockchain's immutability can be leveraged for tracking changes and ensuring the integrity of code and configurations.
7.	**Decentralized Vulnerability Management:**	• Investigate platforms that facilitate decentralized vulnerability reporting, disclosure, and fixing. • Consider leveraging decentralized bug bounty programs for security testing.
8.	**Tokenized Incentives:**	• Explore the possibility of integrating tokenized incentives for identifying and addressing security vulnerabilities. • Research existing blockchain-based platforms that offer reward mechanisms for responsible disclosure.

9. Automated Compliance:	• Investigate how smart contracts can automate compliance checks based on predefined rules and regulations.
10. Monitoring and Incident Response:	• Leverage blockchain's transparency and immutability for real-time monitoring and incident response. • Implement mechanisms to detect unusual transactions or activities on the blockchain.
11. Collaboration and Communication:	• Establish protocols for secure, trustless collaboration between teams using smart contracts. • Use blockchain-based communication tools for secure information sharing.
12. Infrastructure Security:	• Investigate decentralized infrastructure options that offer enhanced security for deploying Web3 applications. • Explore hosting solutions that align with Web3 principles and enhance the overall security posture.

Table 4 **Navigating the Cutting Edge:** Unveiling the Web3 and DevSecOps Synergy with Tools of Tomorrow

As Web3 and DevSecOps continue to shape the landscape as emerging trends, here is a compilation of pertinent tools essential for effectively implementing DevSecOps projects within Web3.

Truffle Suite:	Truffle is a widespread development framework for Ethereum-based projects. It offers tools for compiling, deploying, and testing smart contracts. Truffle also integrates with testing frameworks and supports DevSecOps practices.
Hardhat:	Hardhat is another development environment for Ethereum that provides a wide range of development and testing tools. It's highly extensible and designed to support both development and DevSecOps practices.
Ganache:	Ganache is a personal Ethereum blockchain that developers can use for testing. It helps simulate the Ethereum network locally, allowing software developers to test their smart contracts and dapps in a controlled environment.
OpenZeppelin:	OpenZeppelin provides a library of reusable and secure smart contracts for Ethereum-based projects. It includes various security mechanisms to help developers build more secure smart contracts.
MythX:	MythX is a security analysis platform for Ethereum smart contracts. It can help identify vulnerabilities and security

	issues in the smart contracts by performing static and dynamic analysis.
Solhint and Solium:	These are linters for Solidity, the programming language for Ethereum smart contracts. They help developers follow best practices and avoid potential security vulnerabilities.
Git/GitHub/GitLab:	These version control and code hosting platforms are fundamental for DevSecOps practices. They enable collaboration, version control, and automated workflows.
Jenkins/Travis CI/CircleCI:	These are widespread continuous integration and continuous deployment (CI/CD) tools that can help automate building, testing, and deploying Web3 projects.
Docker:	Docker is a containerization platform that permits the application's package, dependencies, and blockchain components into a container. This ensures consistency across different environments.
Kubernetes:	If you're dealing with complex deployments, Kubernetes can help you orchestrate and manage containerized applications, making it easier to scale and manage Web3 applications.
Security Scanning Tools:	Tools like Snyk, SonarQube, and OWASP ZAP can be used to conduct security scans on the code and smart contracts to identify vulnerabilities.
Monitoring and Analytics:	Tools like Grafana, Prometheus, and ELK stack can help monitor the health and functioning of Web3 applications and blockchain components.

II. Understanding the CI/CD Pipeline

A. Definition and Key Components of the CI/CD Pipeline

The CI/CD pipeline comprises a series of stages that automate the software development process from code changes to deployment. It typically includes the following key components:

Version Control System (VCS): The VCS, such as Git, allows teams to manage code changes, track revisions, and collaborate effectively.

Continuous Integration (CI): This phase involves automatically building and integrating code changes from multiple developers into a shared repository. It includes running unit tests to validate code quality and compatibility.

Continuous Deployment (CD): The CD phase automates deploying applications to different environments, such as development, staging, and production. It ensures that the application is packaged, configured, and deployed consistently.

Testing and Quality Assurance: Various types of testing, such as unit tests, integration tests, and acceptance tests, are performed during the pipeline to verify the functionality and quality of the software.

Artifact Repository: This component stores-built artifacts, such as compiled code or container images, for later use in the deployment phase.

DevSecOps Project Monitoring

Project Name < Enter Project Name> Assessment Week <Select Week> Project Performance

Phase	Score
1. Project Overview	3.67
2. Project Initiation	2.67
3. Requirements Gathering	5.00
4. Design and Architecture	3.67
5. Tool Selection and Setup	2.67
6. Development and Integration	5.00
7. Continuous Security Testing	5.00
8. Infrastructure Security	3.67
9. Documentation and Training	4.00
Project Performance	3.92

Phase	Activity	Deliverables	Responsible	Timeline	Assessment	Score	Assessment Guidelines
1. Project Overview	Define project goals and objectives	Project charter	Project Manager	1 week	5: Excellent progress	5	
	Determine project scope and boundaries	Scope document			4: Good progress	4	
	Identify key stakeholders and their roles	Stakeholder matrix			2: Limited progress	2	
2. Project Initiation	Form project team and assign responsibilities	Project team	Project Manager	1 week	1: Poor or no progress	1	
	Conduct kickoff meeting to establish communication	Meeting minutes			3: Moderate progress	3	
	Define project governance structure	Governance plan			4: Good progress	4	
3. Requirements Gathering	Identify security and compliance requirements	Requirements document	Security Analysts	2 weeks	5: Excellent progress	5	
	Assess existing processes and systems	Process assessment report			5: Excellent progress	5	
	Conduct stakeholder interviews	Interview notes			5: Excellent progress	5	
4. Design and Architecture	Define DevSecOps architecture	Architecture diagram	DevSecOps Lead	3 weeks	5: Excellent progress	5	
	Develop security guidelines and best practices	Security guidelines			4: Good progress	4	
	Design CI/CD pipeline and incorporate security testing at each stage	CI/CD pipeline design			2: Limited progress	2	
5. Tool Selection and Setup	Evaluate and select appropriate tools	Tool selection report	DevSecOps Lead	2 weeks	1: Poor or no progress	1	
	Set up selected tools and configure integrations	Configured tools			3: Moderate progress	3	
	Conduct training for the team on selected tools	Training materials			4: Good progress	4	
6. Development and Integration	Implement secure coding practices	Code repository with secure cod	Development Team	4 weeks	5: Excellent progress	5	
	Incorporate security testing tools in the CI/CD pipeline	CI/CD pipeline with security test			5: Excellent progress	5	
	Integrate security-focused tests into automated testing suite	Automated testing suite with se			5: Excellent progress	5	
7. Continuous Security Testing	Configure and run vulnerability scans	Vulnerability scan reports	Security Analysts	Ongoing	5: Excellent progress	5	
	Implement security monitoring and logging	Monitoring and logging setup			5: Excellent progress	5	
	Integrate static code analysis and software composition analysis tools into the pipeline	Code analysis reports			5: Excellent progress	5	
8. Infrastructure Security	Apply infrastructure-as-code principles	Infrastructure as code template	Infrastructure Team	3 weeks	3: Moderate progress	3	
	Implement automated configuration management and security hardening for infrastructure components	Automated configuration manag			3: Moderate progress	3	
	Regularly assess and remediate security vulnerabilities	Vulnerability remediation report			5: Excellent progress	5	
9. Documentation and Training	Document DevSecOps processes, procedures, and guidelines	Process documentation	Documentation Team	4 weeks	5: Excellent progress	5	
	Create training materials and conduct training	Training materials			3: Moderate progress	3	

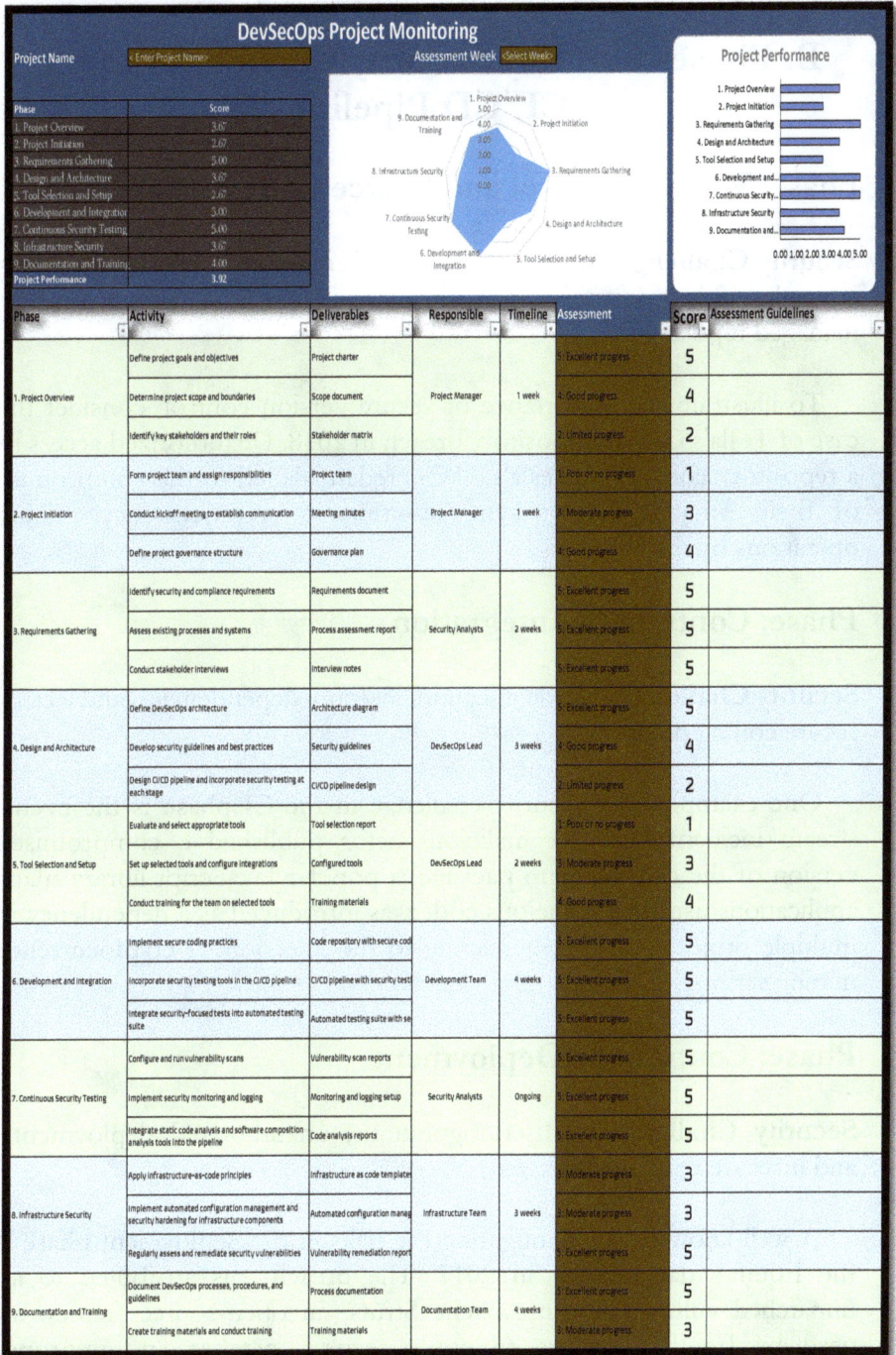

Hands-on tool: Snapshot of Monitoring a DevSecOps Project

B. Phases and Key Security Challenges in the CI/CD Pipeline

Phase: Version Control and Source Code Management

Security Challenges: Insecure storage of credentials, inadequate access controls, and exposure of sensitive information through improperly managed repositories.

To illustrate the importance of secure version control, consider the case of Tesla's GitLab repository breach in 2018. Unauthorized access to a repository containing Tesla's AWS credentials led to the compromise of their Amazon S3 buckets, resulting in cryptocurrency mining operations by the attackers.

Phase: Continuous Integration

Security Challenges: Code injection, insecure dependencies, and lack of secure coding practices.

One example of a security challenge in the CI phase is the event-stream incident 2018. A malicious actor published a compromised version of the event-stream package, a popular JavaScript library many applications use. The malicious code was introduced as a dependency in multiple projects, ultimately leading to the injection of cryptocurrency mining scripts.

Phase: Continuous Deployment

Security Challenges: Misconfigurations, unauthorized deployments, and insecure container images.

A well-known case highlighting the risks in the deployment phase is the Equifax data breach in 2017. The breach was attributed to an unpatched vulnerability in Apache Struts, an open-source framework used by Equifax. Failure to apply security patches and improper deployment practices led to unauthorized access and the theft of sensitive consumer data.

By understanding the phases and associated security challenges in the CI/CD pipeline, organizations can proactively implement security measures at each stage to mitigate risks effectively.

Table 5 **Behind the Firewall:** Unveiling Cybersecurity Chronicles

Consider a software development company that uses Jenkins as its CI/CD tool. They face the challenge of ensuring the security of their CI/CD pipeline. Here's how they address some of the security challenges:

Potential security challenge	Potential solution	Practical examples:
Vulnerability management: Ensuring software dependencies in the CI/CD pipeline are free from known vulnerabilities.	Regularly implement automated vulnerability scanning tools, checking for vulnerabilities in third-party libraries and components. For example, it uses tools like OWASP.	The company integrates a vulnerability scanning tool, such as OWASP Dependency Check, into its pipeline. This tool automatically scans their codebase for known vulnerabilities in open-source libraries and provides alerts or fails the build if critical vulnerabilities are detected.
Code integrity and authentication: Verify the source code's authenticity and integrity during the CI/CD process to prevent unauthorized modifications.	Utilize version control systems and digital signatures to track changes to the codebase and ensure its authenticity. For instance, it uses Git for version control and implementing code signing to verify the integrity of the code.	The company enforces version control (e.g., Git) and implements code signing. They require all commits to be digitally signed, ensuring the authenticity and integrity of the codebase.
Credential and secrets management: Safeguarding sensitive information such as API keys, database credentials, or encryption keys used in the CI/CD pipeline.	Utilize secure storage solutions like HashiCorp Vault or AWS Secrets Manager to store and manage secrets securely. Implement access controls and encryption to protect sensitive information.	The company has adopted a secret management solution like HashiCorp Vault. They securely store and manage sensitive information in the vault, such as API keys and database credentials. The CI/CD pipeline retrieves the required secrets dynamically during the build or deployment process, minimizing exposure.

Infrastructure security: Ensuring the security of the infrastructure supporting the CI/CD pipeline, including servers, containers, and orchestration systems.	Implement secure infrastructure configurations using tools like Terraform or CloudFormation templates with hardened security controls. Regularly patch and update the infrastructure components to mitigate vulnerabilities.	The company utilizes infrastructure-as-code (IaC) tools like Terraform or CloudFormation. They maintain hardened security configurations and regularly update their infrastructure components to patch vulnerabilities. They also implement continuous vulnerability scanning for their infrastructure using tools like AWS Inspector.
Continuous monitoring: Having visibility into the CI/CD pipeline and detecting security issues in real-time.	Implement monitoring and logging solutions like Prometheus, ELK stack, or Splunk to capture and analyze logs, metrics, and events from the CI/CD pipeline. Set up alerts and notifications for potential security incidents.	The company integrates monitoring and logging tools like Prometheus and the ELK stack. They collect and analyze logs and metrics from the CI/CD pipeline, enabling real-time detection of security incidents. They set up alerts and notifications to respond promptly to any security issues.

By addressing these challenges with the mentioned potential solutions and utilizing appropriate tools, the team can enhance the security of its CI/CD pipeline, reducing the risk of security breaches or vulnerabilities in its software releases.

III. DevSecOps Principles and Benefits

A. Explanation of DevSecOps and Its Core Principles

DevSecOps integrates security practices seamlessly into the CI/CD pipeline to address security concerns early and consistently. It promotes collaboration, communication, and shared responsibility among development, security, and operations teams. The core principles of DevSecOps include the following:

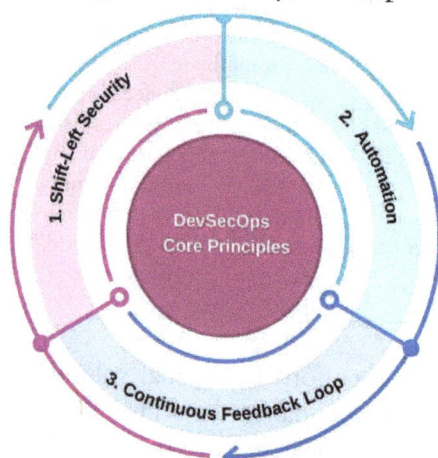

Shift-Left Security: Emphasizes addressing security requirements and considerations in the software development lifecycle as early as possible. By integrating security, organizations can identify and address vulnerabilities early, reducing potential risks and associated costs.

Automation: Automation plays a crucial role in DevSecOps by enabling consistent security checks, continuous monitoring, and rapid response to security incidents. Automated security testing, vulnerability scanning, and deployment processes help maintain the integrity and security of the pipeline.

Continuous Feedback Loop: DevSecOps promotes a feedback-driven approach, where information about security vulnerabilities, threats, and incidents is shared transparently among teams. This feedback loop ensures that security concerns are promptly addressed and lessons learned from previous incidents are applied to improve overall security posture.

Table 6 **Unburdening the Codebase:** Proven Tips to Tackle Technical Debt

Technical debt in the DevSecOps toolchain refers to the accumulated consequences of design or implementation choices that prioritize immediate gains or quick solutions over long-term maintainability, scalability, and security. This debt builds up over time and can harm the toolchain's development speed, operational efficiency, and security.

To address technical debt in the DevSecOps toolchain, allocating resources, time, and effort to refactor, upgrade, automate, and streamline its components is essential. By doing so, we can ensure long-term maintainability, scalability, and security. Technical debt in the toolchain can manifest in various ways, and it is crucial to identify and tackle these issues to mitigate risks and enhance the overall effectiveness of our DevSecOps practices.

Outdated or Deprecated Versions:	Using obsolete versions of tools, libraries, or frameworks in the toolchain can lead to security vulnerabilities, compatibility issues, and limited access to new features or improvements.
Inefficient or Inconsistent Configurations:	Inadequate or inconsistent configurations of tools and components can hinder performance, impact security, and increase maintenance efforts.
Lack of Automation:	Insufficient automation in the toolchain can result in manual processes, increased risk of human error, slower deployments, and difficulty maintaining consistent security controls across the pipeline.
Redundant or Overlapping Tools:	Unnecessary duplication of tools or overlapping functionality within the toolchain can introduce complexity, increase maintenance efforts, and lead to consistency.
Insufficient Testing and Monitoring:	Inadequate testing or monitoring mechanisms can leave vulnerabilities undetected, impair the ability to identify and address issues promptly, and undermine the overall security posture of the pipeline.
Inconsistent Security Practices:	Inconsistencies in applying security practices across the toolchain, such as weak access controls, inadequate encryption, or insecure default

	configurations, can introduce security vulnerabilities.
Lack of Documentation and Knowledge Sharing:	Insufficient documentation, knowledge sharing, and inadequate training can impede effective maintenance, troubleshooting, and onboarding processes, leading to longer response times and increased technical debt.

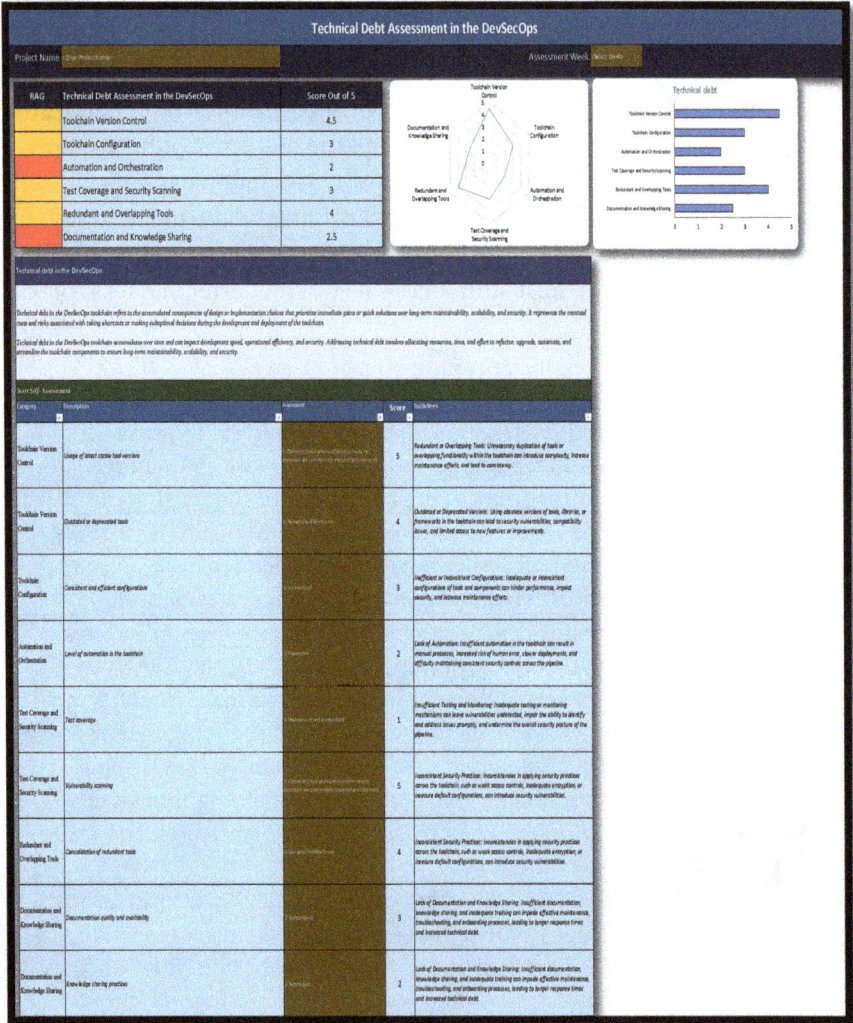

Hands-on tool: Snapshot of Technical Debt

B. Integration of Security into the CI/CD Pipeline

DevSecOps advocates for integrating security activities at each CI/CD pipeline stage. This includes:

- **Security Testing:** Incorporating automated security testing, such as dynamic application security testing (DAST), static application security testing (SAST), and software composition analysis (SCA), to identify vulnerabilities and weaknesses in the codebase and dependencies.

- **Infrastructure as Code (IaC):** Applying safe coding practices and security controls to the infrastructure definition files used in the deployment process. Tools like Terraform and CloudFormation can ensure consistent security configurations across environments.

- **Secure Image Creation:** Implementing safe container image creation processes, including vulnerability scanning of base images, secure configuration of container runtimes, and regular patching to prevent known vulnerabilities.

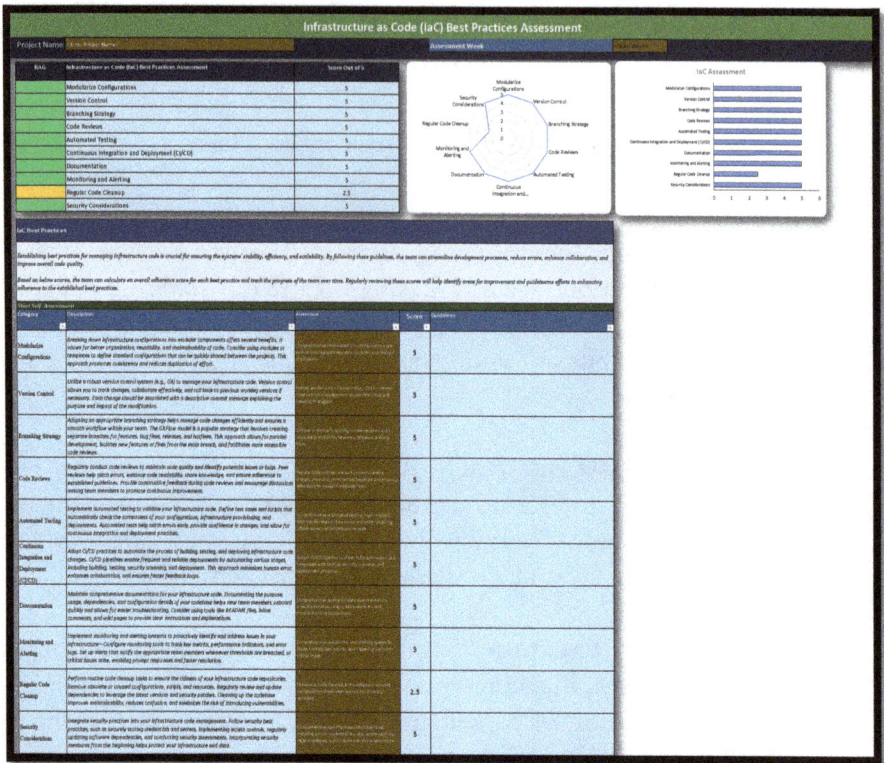

Hands-on tool: Snapshot of Best practices in IaC

Table 7 **Infrastructure as Code (IaC):** Harnessing Best Practices for Seamless Deployments

Best Practice	Description
Modularize Configurations:	Breaking down infrastructure configurations into modular components offers several benefits. It allows for better organization, reusability, and maintainability of code. Consider using modules or templates to define standard configurations that can be quickly shared between the projects. This approach promotes consistency and reduces duplication of effort.
Version Control:	Utilize a robust version control system (e.g., Git) to manage your infrastructure code. Version control allows you to track changes, collaborate effectively, and roll back to previous working versions if necessary. Each change should be associated with a descriptive commit message explaining the purpose and impact of the modification.

Branching Strategy:	Adopting an appropriate branching strategy helps manage code changes efficiently and ensures a smooth workflow within your team. The GitFlow model is a popular strategy that involves creating separate branches for features, bug fixes, releases, and hotfixes. This approach allows for parallel development, isolates new features or fixes from the main branch, and facilitates more accessible code reviews.
Code Reviews:	Regularly conduct code reviews to maintain code quality and identify potential issues or bugs. Peer reviews help catch errors, enhance code readability, share knowledge, and ensure adherence to established guidelines. Provide constructive feedback during code reviews and encourage discussions among team members to promote continuous improvement.
Automated Testing:	Implement automated testing to validate your infrastructure code. Define test cases and scripts that automatically check the correctness of your configurations, infrastructure provisioning, and deployments. Automated tests help catch errors early, provide confidence in changes, and allow continuous integration and deployment practices.
Continuous Integration and Deployment (CI/CD):	Adopt CI/CD practices to automate the process of building, testing, and deploying infrastructure code changes. CI/CD pipelines enable frequent and reliable deployments by automating various stages, including building, testing, security scanning, and deployment. This approach minimizes human error, enhances collaboration, and ensures faster feedback loops.
Documentation:	Maintain comprehensive documentation for your infrastructure code. Documenting your codebase's purpose, usage, dependencies, and configuration details helps new team members onboard quickly and allows easier troubleshooting. Use tools like README files, inline comments, and wiki pages to provide clear instructions and explanations.
Monitoring and Alerting:	Implement monitoring and alerting systems to proactively identify and address issues in your infrastructure—Configure monitoring tools to track key metrics, performance indicators, and error logs. Set up alerts that notify the appropriate team members whenever thresholds are breached, or critical issues arise, enabling prompt responses and faster resolution.
Regular Code Cleanup:	Perform routine code cleanup tasks to ensure the tidiness of your infrastructure code repositories. Remove obsolete or unused configurations, scripts, and resources. Regularly review and update dependencies to leverage the latest versions and security patches. Cleaning up the codebase

	improves maintainability, reduces confusion, and minimizes the risk of introducing vulnerabilities.
Security Considerations:	Integrate security practices into your infrastructure code management. Follow security best practices, such as securely storing credentials and secrets, implementing access controls, regularly updating software dependencies, and conducting security assessments. Incorporating security measures from the beginning helps protect your infrastructure and data.

C. Benefits of Implementing DevSecOps Practices

Implementing DevSecOps practices brings several benefits to organizations:

- **Improved Security Posture:** By integrating security throughout the CI/CD pipeline, organizations can proactively identify and remediate vulnerabilities, reducing the likelihood of successful attacks and data breaches.

- **Faster Remediation:** Automated security testing and continuous monitoring enable early detection of vulnerabilities, allowing developers to address them quickly and efficiently. This minimizes the time required to fix security issues and enhances software delivery speed.

- **Enhanced Collaboration:** DevSecOps fosters collaboration between development, security, and operations teams. By breaking down silos and encouraging cross-functional communication, teams can identify security risks, share knowledge, and improve the pipeline's security.

- **Cost Efficiency:** Early detection and remediation of security vulnerabilities reduce the potential financial impact of security incidents. Moreover, incorporating security practices early in development minimizes the need for expensive post-deployment fixes.

By embracing DevSecOps, organizations can establish a culture of security and resilience, aligning the interests of different teams and ensuring a robust CI/CD pipeline that prioritizes safety without compromising development velocity.

Table 8 **The Vulnerability Lifecycle:** A Proactive Process for Tracking and Addressing Security Risks

Tracking and addressing vulnerabilities disclosed in software components is crucial to maintaining the security of your software. Here are some of the best processes to effectively handle vulnerabilities:

Step	Description
1. **Establish a Vulnerability Management Process**	Create a well-defined process for managing vulnerabilities, including identification, assessment, and remediation steps. Define roles, responsibilities, and escalation procedures.
2. **Stay Informed**	Stay updated on security advisories, vulnerability databases, and relevant mailing lists to receive timely alerts about disclosed vulnerabilities.
3. **Assess Vulnerability Severity**	Evaluate the severity and potential impact of each disclosed vulnerability. Prioritize vulnerabilities based on risk level and criticality of the affected software component.
4. **Perform Risk Analysis**	Conduct a risk analysis considering the likelihood of exploitation, presence of mitigating controls, and sensitivity of the information at risk.
5. **Patch Management**	Establish a patch management process to apply security patches and updates. Create a schedule based on vulnerability severity and availability of patches.
6. **Remediation Planning**	Develop a detailed plan for addressing each identified vulnerability, including necessary actions, required resources, and a timeline for remediation.
7. **Patch Validation and Testing**	Thoroughly test patches and updates in a testing environment similar to production. Identify issues, conflicts, or regressions before deployment.
8. **Implement Security Controls**	Apply compensating security controls to mitigate risk until vulnerabilities are patched. Examples include network segmentation and intrusion detection systems.
9. **Incident Response Planning**	Include vulnerability management in the incident response plan. Define steps, procedures, communication channels, and coordination with stakeholders.
10. **Continuous Monitoring**	Implement continuous monitoring mechanisms such as vulnerability scanning, log analysis, and intrusion detection systems to identify vulnerabilities proactively.
11. **Vendor Relationships**	Maintain effective relationships with vendors to understand their vulnerability management processes and responsiveness in addressing disclosed vulnerabilities.

12. **Engage in the Community**	Participate in security communities, forums, and bug bounty programs to gain insights, make responsible disclosures, and collaborate on fixes.
13. **Establish a Security Culture**	Foster a culture of security within the teams. Promote security awareness, knowledge sharing, and proactive identification of vulnerabilities.
14. **Security Testing and Reviews**	Implement regular security testing, code reviews, and automated security scanning to identify vulnerabilities early in development.
15. **Document and Track**	Maintain a centralized system to track vulnerabilities, their status, and corresponding remediation efforts: document actions taken and risk acceptance decisions.

D. Securing Software Delivery: A Step-by-Step Guide to DevSecOps Implementation

Implementing DevSecOps requires careful planning and a step-by-step approach to successfully incorporate security procedures into the software development and operations processes. Here is a practical industry-acceptable guide for DevSecOps implementation strategy:

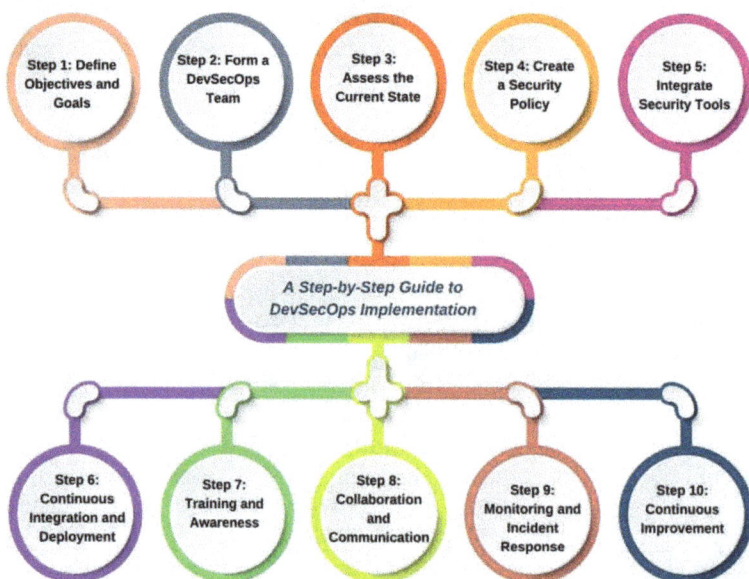

Step 1: Define Objectives and Goals
* Clearly define the objectives and goals of your DevSecOps implementation.

- Identify the security requirements and compliance standards specific to your industry.

Step 2: Form a DevSecOps Team
- Assemble a cross-functional team that includes development, operations, and security representatives.
- Appoint a DevSecOps champion to lead the implementation efforts.

Step 3: Assess the Current State
- Conduct a thorough assessment of your current development and operations processes.
- Identify security gaps, vulnerabilities, and areas for improvement.
- Perform a risk assessment to prioritize security requirements.

Step 4: Create a Security Policy
- Develop a thorough security policy that outlines the security principles and guidelines for the entire development lifecycle.
- Include security controls, access management, encryption, vulnerability management, and incident response processes.

Step 5: Integrate Security Tools
- Evaluate and select appropriate security tools that align with your objectives and goals.
- Examples include static code analysis, vulnerability scanning, security testing frameworks, and threat intelligence platforms.
- Integrate these tools into your development and operations workflows.

Step 6: Continuous Integration and Deployment
- Implement a continuous integration and deployment (CI/CD) pipeline.
- Automate build, test, and deployment processes to ensure consistent and secure software delivery.
- Integrate security checks at each pipeline stage, such as automated security testing and vulnerability scanning.

Step 7: Training and Awareness
- Provide training and awareness programs for the development, operations, and security teams.

- Educate team members on secure coding practices, security vulnerabilities, and incident response procedures.

Step 8: Collaboration and Communication
- Foster collaboration and communication between development, operations, and security teams.
- Encourage the sharing of information, knowledge, and best practices.
- Implement tools and platforms that facilitate communication and collaboration.

Step 9: Monitoring and Incident Response
- Implement a strong monitoring technique to detect and respond to security incidents.
- Use intrusion detection systems, log analysis tools, and security information and event management (SIEM) solutions.
- Define incident response procedures and establish a dedicated response team.

Step 10: Continuous Improvement
- Regularly assess and review your DevSecOps implementation.
- Collect metrics and feedback to measure the effectiveness of security practices.
- Continuously refine and improve your DevSecOps processes based on lessons learned.
- DevSecOps is an ongoing journey; continuous improvement is critical to its success. Adapt the steps based on your organization's specific needs and requirements.

Table 9 **From Vulnerability to Victory:** Safeguarding Systems with Safe Coding Practices

Adhere to established coding standards such as OWASP Top 10, CWE/SANS Top 25, and CERT secure coding guidelines. Follow language-specific secure coding practices and frameworks.

Secure Coding Standards:	
Secure Development Lifecycle (SDLC):	Implement a comprehensive SDLC that includes security considerations from the initial design phase to deployment and maintenance. Integrate security activities into every stage of the development process.
Threat Modeling:	Perform threat modeling exercises to identify potential security risks and vulnerabilities in the system. This helps prioritize security efforts and implement appropriate safeguards.
Secure Dependencies:	Validate and sanitize all user inputs to prevent common attacks by SQL injection, cross-site scripting (XSS), and command injection. Use secure input validation libraries and frameworks.
Executive Order on Improving the Nation's Cybersecurity (applicable to the United States of America)	The "Executive Order on Improving the Nation's Cybersecurity" is a presidential directive designed to strengthen the country's cybersecurity infrastructure and response capabilities. This order is a comprehensive plan that primarily targets the enhancement of cybersecurity within the federal government, cooperation with the private sector, and fostering international collaboration. Its main objectives revolve around modernizing, standardizing, and fortifying the nation's defenses against cyber threats. The President of the United States signed this policy directive on May 12, 2021.
Authentication and Authorization:	Implement robust authentication mechanisms, such as multi-factor authentication (MFA), and enforce proper authorization controls to safeguard that only approved users can access sensitive data and functionality.
Secure Configuration Management:	Securely manage configuration files, secrets, and credentials. Avoid hardcoding sensitive information in source code and version control systems. Use secure storage and management solutions like vaults or critical management systems.

Encryption:	Implement appropriate encryption techniques for data at rest and in transit. Use industry-standard encryption algorithms and secure critical management practices. Ensure that sensitive information is not exposed unintentionally.
Logging and Monitoring:	Implement comprehensive logging and monitoring mechanisms to detect and respond to security events and anomalies. Collect logs from various system components and establish a centralized log management system.
Secure Deployment Practices:	Employ secure deployment techniques, such as immutable infrastructure and containerization, to ensure consistent and secure deployment of applications. Automate deployment processes using secure CI/CD pipelines.
Continuous Security Testing:	Conduct regular security assessments, vulnerability scans, and penetration testing to identify and remediate security weaknesses. Implement automated security testing as part of your CI/CD pipeline.
Incident Response Planning:	Develop an incident response plan to define the steps and procedures for responding to security incidents. Regularly test and upgrade the plan to ensure its effectiveness.
Security Awareness and Training:	Provide ongoing security awareness and training programs for developers and other stakeholders to enhance their understanding of secure coding practices and emerging threats.
Peer Code Reviews:	Implement a code review process that includes security-focused reviews. Encourage developers to review each other's code for security vulnerabilities, adherence to secure coding standards, and best practices.
Secure Third-Party Integrations:	Evaluate the security posture of third-party services, APIs, and libraries before integrating them into your application. Consider their security track record, documentation, and ongoing support.
Secure Data Handling:	Implement appropriate measures to protect sensitive data, such as secure storage, anonymization, and minimization. Follow privacy regulations and best practices for data protection.
Patch Management:	Establish a process for timely patch management to address security vulnerabilities in the underlying infrastructure, operating systems, and applications. Regularly update systems and test patches before deployment.

Security Testing Environments:	Set up dedicated security testing environments that mimic production environments closely. Perform security testing in controlled environments, including penetration and vulnerability assessments.
Secure APIs:	Apply secure coding practices when designing and developing APIs. Implement authentication, authorization, input validation, and rate-limiting mechanisms to protect against common API attacks.
Regular Security Assessments:	Perform regular security assessments and audits to ensure compliance with relevant security standards, regulations, and policies. Use external security experts if necessary.

Note: The above practices provide a general guideline for secure coding in a DevSecOps environment. Tailoring these practices to your specific development processes, technology stack, and security requirements is essential.

IV. Best Practices for Securing the CI/CD Pipeline

Securing the Continuous Integration/Continuous Deployment (CI/CD) pipeline is crucial for organizations that strive for efficient software development while maintaining a solid security posture. The CI/CD pipeline automates application build, testing, and deployment, making it a prime target for malicious actors seeking to exploit vulnerabilities. By implementing best practices for securing the CI/CD pipeline, organizations can ensure the integrity, confidentiality, and availability of their software delivery process. This section presents a comprehensive set of best practices to fortify the CI/CD pipeline against potential security threats.

Title	Description	Next Steps
1. Threat Modeling and Risk Assessment	Conduct threat modeling and risk assessments to identify potential threats, vulnerabilities, and their impact on the pipeline's security.	Performing a threat modeling exercise to identify risks and vulnerabilities specific to the CI/CD pipeline, such as unauthorized code deployments or compromised build artifacts.
2. Implementing Secure Coding Practices	Follow secure coding practices to prevent common vulnerabilities like XSS, SQL injection, and insecure deserialization.	Implementing input validation, output encoding, parameterized queries, and utilizing security libraries like OWASP ESAPI or secure coding frameworks like Spring Security.
3. Continuous Vulnerability Scanning and Assessment	Regularly scan for vulnerabilities in code dependencies, libraries, and container images and establish processes to address them.	Integrating vulnerability scanning tools like Snyk, Sonatype Nexus, or Anchore into the CI/CD pipeline to detect and remediate vulnerabilities at build time.
4. Securing the Build and Deployment Processes	Ensure the security of the build and deployment processes, including maintaining secure build environments, signing build artifacts, and validating deployment configurations.	Utilize build systems like Jenkins or GitLab CI/CD to enforce secure build environments and use cryptographic signatures to verify the integrity of build artifacts.

5. Implementing Access Controls and Privilege Management	Enforce access controls, such as RBAC, and manage privileges to prevent unauthorized CI/CD pipeline and resource access.	Implementing fine-grained access controls, multi-factor authentication, and role-based permissions to limit access to critical CI/CD components like deployment scripts or production environments.
6. Monitoring and Logging for Security Incidents	Implement comprehensive monitoring and logging capabilities to detect and respond to security incidents effectively.	Collecting and analyzing logs from CI/CD tools, infrastructure, and runtime environments using tools like ELK Stack, Splunk, or Datadog for proactive threat detection and incident response.
7. Performing Regular Security Testing and Code Reviews	Conduct regular security testing, including penetration testing, vulnerability assessments, and code reviews, to identify and address vulnerabilities.	Conducting periodic penetration testing to identify vulnerabilities in the CI/CD infrastructure and applications and performing manual and automated code reviews for security flaws.
8. Ensuring Secure Configuration Management	Maintain secure configuration management by establishing baselines, enforcing safe defaults, and monitoring for configuration drift.	Applying configuration management tools like Ansible, Puppet, or Chef to enforce consistent and secure configurations for CI/CD tools, cloud infrastructure, and runtime environments.
9. Incorporating Secure Third-Party Dependencies	Carefully evaluate and vet the security of third-party dependencies and regularly update them to mitigate potential risks.	Regularly review and update third-party libraries, frameworks, and modules and utilize dependency management tools like npm, Maven, or pip to detect and remediate vulnerabilities in dependencies.
10. Secure Secrets Management	Implement secure storage and handling of secrets, such as API keys, passwords, and encryption keys, within the CI/CD pipeline.	Utilize secret management tools like HashiCorp Vault or Secrets Manager to securely store and retrieve AWS secrets and avoid hardcoding secrets in code repositories or building configurations.

11. Implementing Infrastructure as Code (IaC) Security	Apply security practices to the infrastructure-as-code (IaC) templates and configuration files used in the CI/CD pipeline.	Utilizing tools like Terraform, CloudFormation, or Kubernetes Security Contexts to enforce secure configurations, manage access controls, and scan for vulnerabilities in infrastructure code.
12. Disaster Recovery and Backup Strategies	Implement disaster recovery plans and backup strategies to ensure business continuity in case of CI/CD pipeline disruptions or data loss.	Regularly back up CI/CD configurations, build artifacts and deployment scripts, and test restoration processes to recover the pipeline in case of failures or data loss.
13. Employee Education and Awareness	Conduct regular security training and awareness programs for CI/CD pipeline users and developers to promote secure practices and raise awareness about emerging threats.	Provide security awareness sessions, conduct phishing simulations, and offer training on secure coding practices and secure use of CI/CD tools.
13. Pipeline Bill of Materials (PBOM)	A Pipeline Bill of Materials (PBOM) is a comprehensive document that outlines all the essential components, tools, and resources necessary for the functioning of your CI/CD pipeline. It serves as a compass that guides you through the labyrinth of technology, ensuring transparency, consistency, and resilience. Think of it as the blueprint for flourishing your development and deployment processes.	See section A. Mastering the CI/CD Symphony: The PBOM Playbook.

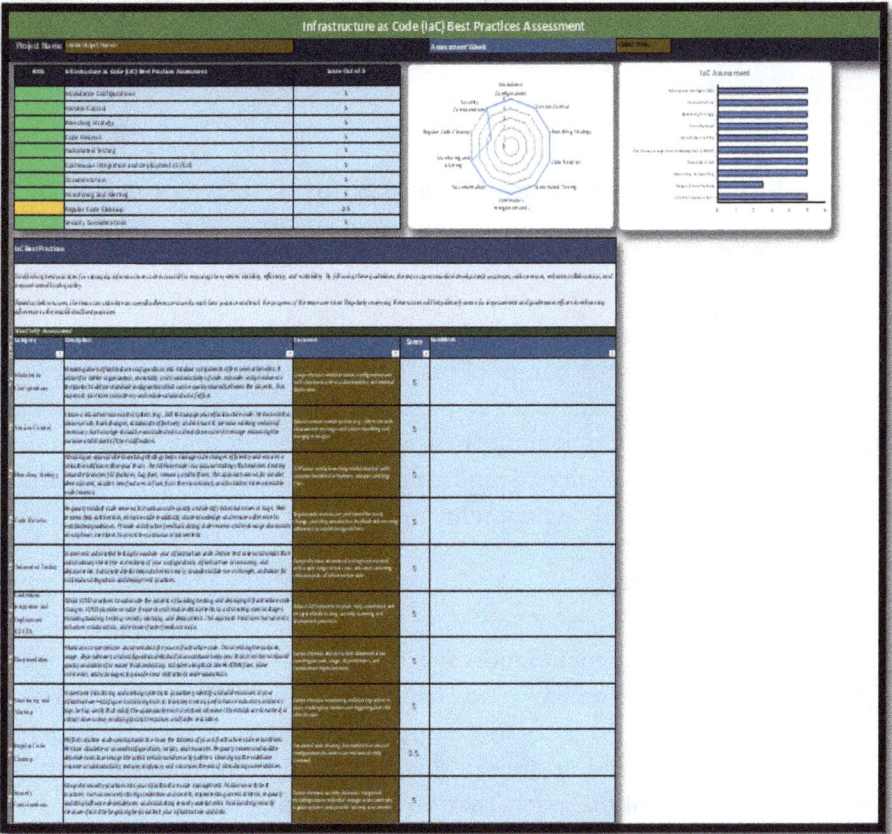

Hands-on tool: Snapshot of Best practices in IaC

A. Mastering the CI/CD Symphony: The PBOM Playbook

Your Path to Pipeline Excellence

The Essential Guide to a Pipeline Bill of Materials (PBOM) for Your CI/CD Pipeline

Introduction: In the dynamic world of modern software development, a solid and efficient Continuous Integration/Continuous Deployment (CI/CD) pipeline is the linchpin of success. This critical component ensures that software is developed, tested, and deployed seamlessly, fostering faster delivery, higher quality, and increased agility. However, creating and maintaining a "Pipeline Bill of Materials" (PBOM) is imperative to achieve these goals. This is often overlooked but plays a crucial role in orchestrating the complex symphony of your CI/CD pipeline.

The PBOM: A Necessity for Modern Software Development

What is a PBOM?

A Pipeline Bill of Materials (PBOM) is a comprehensive document that outlines all the essential components, tools, and resources necessary for the functioning of your CI/CD pipeline. It serves as a compass that guides you through the labyrinth of technology, ensuring transparency, consistency, and resilience. Think of it as the blueprint for flourishing your development and deployment processes.

Why is a PBOM Necessary?

The software development landscape constantly evolves, with new tools and technologies emerging regularly. This rapid evolution makes it challenging to keep track of the components of your CI/CD pipeline accurately. The PBOM addresses this challenge by providing an up-to-date inventory of all the assets that power your pipeline.

Maintaining Your PBOM

Regular Review and Updates

Your PBOM should not be a stagnant document but a living resource that evolves as your CI/CD pipeline evolves. Regular reviews and updates are imperative to ensure that the document remains relevant. The project team should establish the frequency of these reviews based on the pace of changes in the pipeline.

Version Management

In a dynamic environment, maintaining a history of changes is essential. The PBOM should include version management, allowing you to track the evolution of your CI/CD pipeline. By documenting changes over time, you'll have a valuable reference for making informed decisions, troubleshooting, and auditing purposes.

Benefits of a Well-Maintained PBOM

Clarity and Transparency

A well-maintained PBOM ensures an unmistakable understanding of your CI/CD pipeline. Team members and stakeholders can readily access information about the technology stack, tools, and resources. This transparency promotes trust and understanding among all parties involved.

Consistency and Efficiency

Consistency in toolsets and configurations is a cornerstone of a reliable CI/CD pipeline. With a PBOM, you can ensure everyone follows the same set of tools and practices. This consistency streamlines the development and deployment process and reduces the risk of errors and conflicts.

Reference for Stakeholders

The PBOM is not only a technical document; it's also a valuable reference for stakeholders who may not be deeply involved in the technical aspects of your CI/CD pipeline. Executives, project managers, and clients can gain insights into the technology stack and the resources required for development and deployment.

Promoting a Culture of Accountability

Maintaining an up-to-date PBOM instills a culture of accountability within the project team. It encourages ownership of components and ensures that any changes or updates are well-documented and communicated. This accountability contributes to a smoother and more dictated development and deployment process.

In modern software development, a Pipeline Bill of Materials (PBOM) is not a mere formality but a vital tool for success. It empowers you to navigate the complexity of your CI/CD pipeline while fostering transparency, consistency, and efficiency. By regularly reviewing and updating your PBOM, you ensure that your development and deployment processes stay aligned with your evolving needs and the dynamic landscape of software development. In essence, the PBOM is the backbone that keeps your CI/CD pipeline solid and agile, enabling you to deliver high-quality software faster and more effectively.

PBOM Benefits:

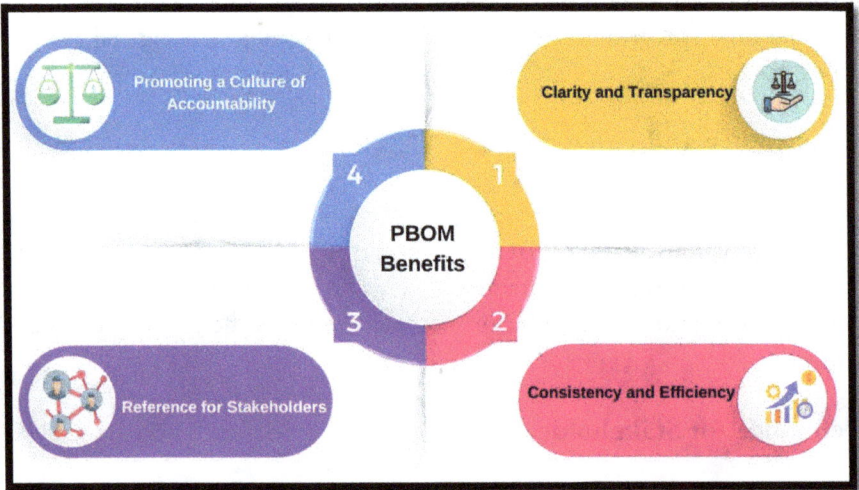

CI/CD Pipeline Bill of Material (PBOM):

CI/CD PIPELINE BILL OF MATERIAL (PBOM)

A CI/CD (Continuous Integration/Continuous Deployment) pipeline serves as an integral component of contemporary software development. Creating a 'Pipeline Bill of Material' (PBOM) is crucial in meticulously cataloging all the components and tools necessary for the pipeline's operation. Maintaining a routine schedule for reviewing and updating the PBOM is imperative to keep pace with the evolving pipeline and shifting requirements. The responsibility of determining the update frequency and managing prior versions of the PBOM falls upon the project team. The PBOM stands as a comprehensive inventory of components, tools, and resources indispensable for the seamless functioning of your CI/CD pipeline. Its purpose is to ensure a crystal-clear comprehension of your technology stack and the available resources for development and deployment. The timely upkeep of the PBOM is paramount, especially as new tools or components are integrated. It functions as an invaluable point of reference for all stakeholders involved in the software development process, fostering transparency and consistency in the operation of the pipeline.

1 Pipeline Overview	2 Version Control System (VCS)	3 Continuous Integration (CI) Server
Project Name	Repository	Server Tool
Description < pipeline is associated with > < goals of the pipeline >	Branching Strategy < repository > < being used (e.g. Gitflow, GitHub Flow) >	Configuration Files < versions, Travis CI > < .jenkinsfile, .travis.yml >

4 Build and Compilation:	5 Testing Frameworks	6 Artifact Repository
Build Tools	Unit Testing	Repository Manager < Artifactory >
Compiler/Interpreter & Docker Images	Integration Testing & Code Quality	Artifacts
Compiler/Interpreter < Specify the language and version being used (e.g., Node.js, Java 11) >	Integration Testing < tools and frameworks for integration testing >	< Include what gets stored, such as JAR files, Docker images, etc. >
Docker Images < If containerization is used, specify Docker images and their versions. >	Code Quality < Specify static code analysis tools (e.g., SonarQube, ESLint). >	

7 Deployment Targets	8 Deployment Tools	9 Monitoring and Logging
Staging Environment	Orchestration	Monitoring Tools < health and performance >
Production Environment < Describe the production environment setup. >	Deployment Scripts < deployments (e.g., Kubernetes, Docker Swarm). >	Logging Tools < logging/log aggregation tools in use >

10 Notification and Alerts:	11 Security Scanning	12 Backup and Rollback
Notification Services	Vulnerability Scanning	Backup Strategy < Define the backup mechanisms in place >
Alerting Policies < ment (e.g., Slack, email). > < for issues >	Security Testing < dependencies. > < ing practices. >	Rollback Plan < when it's possible a version in case of issues. >

13 Documentation	14 Access Control	15 Compliance and Regulations
CI/CD Pipeline Documentation	User Access	Compliance
Deployment Documentation < pipeline setup and usage. > < ... >	Credentials Management < ... pipeline. > < ... handled? >	Compliance Requirements < regulations > < Mention any relevant specific of regulatory compliance requirements (e.g., GDPR, HIPAA.) >

16 Dependencies and Licenses	17 Maintenance and Upkeep	18 Disaster Recovery
List of Dependencies	Schedule Tasks	Business Continuity < ... Disaster Recovery >
License Information < third-party components. >	Updates & Patches < ... es. > < ... handled? >	Disaster Recovery Plan < Business Continuity > < recovering from major outages or data loss. >

19 Support and Contacts	20 Change Management	21 Training and Support
Support and Contracts	Change Approvers	Training Needs
On-call Schedule < ... d questions. >	Change Control Process < Describe the process for introducing changes to the pipeline. >	Training & Support < Training resources for the team - Support and troubleshooting documentation. >

22 Workflow and Process Documentation	23 Costs and Budget	24 Sign Off & Approvers
Documentation	Cost Approvers & Schedule	Approvers < reviewers who need to approve >
Workflow Diagrams < repository > < Process documentation for CI/CD stages >	Cost Estimation < schedules > < Estimate the costs associated with maintaining the CI/CD pipeline. >	Sign Off < CI/CD Pipeline Bill of Material (PBOM) > < Attach Evidences of Approvals along with Dates >

55

V. Automation and Tooling for Pipeline Security

A. The Dynamic Duo of Automation and Tooling in DevSecOps

In the ever-evolving world of software development, the marriage of Development (Dev) and Security (Sec) has given birth to a transformative approach known as DevSecOps. At its core, DevSecOps aims to integrate security practices seamlessly into the development lifecycle, ensuring the rapid delivery of secure and reliable software. However, the true catalyst for this paradigm shift is the dynamic duo of automation and tooling. This article explores the exciting realm of automation and tooling in DevSecOps, unraveling its significance, benefits, and how it propels organizations toward achieving security and operational excellence.

Unleashing the Power of Automation:

Automation has emerged as the backbone of DevSecOps, revolutionizing how software is developed, tested, deployed, and monitored. By automating repetitive and manual tasks, developers and security professionals can focus their efforts on more critical and creative endeavors. Imagine a world where mundane tasks, like vulnerability scanning, configuration management, and compliance checks, are efficiently handled by automated processes, freeing up valuable time and resources.

Benefits of Automation in DevSecOps:

1. **Enhanced Efficiency:** Automation eliminates human error and accelerates the development lifecycle. With automated testing, deployments, and security checks, organizations can achieve faster time-to-market without compromising quality or security.

2. **Consistency and Standardization:** Automation ensures that processes and configurations are consistently applied throughout the

software development lifecycle. This promotes better collaboration, reduces inconsistencies, and helps meet compliance requirements.

3. **Continuous Security:** By integrating automated security practices into every stage of development, from code scanning to vulnerability management, organizations can proactively address security risks and ensure a robust security posture.

4. **Scalability:** Automation enables organizations to scale their operations seamlessly. It empowers teams to handle complex environments, multiple deployments, and diverse application architectures.

Tooling: The Enabler of DevSecOps Excellence:

While automation provides the foundation, the comprehensive suite of tools amplifies the capabilities and effectiveness of DevSecOps practices. From code analysis and continuous integration to vulnerability scanning and container security, many tools are available that cater to specific needs throughout the development lifecycle.

Benefits of Tooling in DevSecOps:

1. **Comprehensive Security Coverage:** DevSecOps tooling empowers organizations to identify vulnerabilities, detect threats, and enforce security policies at every stage of development. This ensures that security is not an afterthought but an integral part of the process.

2. **Real-Time Monitoring and Alerting:** DevSecOps tools enable continuous monitoring of application performance, infrastructure, and security metrics. This real-time visibility allows teams to identify and respond to potential security incidents promptly.

3. **Streamlined Collaboration:** Tooling promotes collaboration among development, operations, and security teams by providing a platform for sharing information, tracking issues, and facilitating communication. This leads to faster incident response and improved overall productivity.

4. **Compliance and Audit Readiness:** DevSecOps tools assist organizations in meeting regulatory compliance requirements by automating security checks, generating audit reports, and providing visibility into security controls.

Automation and tooling are the backbone of successful DevSecOps implementations, enabling organizations to achieve higher efficiency, security, and agility levels. Embracing automation reduces human error, accelerates processes, and allows teams to focus on innovation. The right combination of DevSecOps tools provides comprehensive security coverage, streamlines collaboration, and ensures compliance with industry standards.

In the ever-evolving landscape of software development, organizations that embrace the power of automation and tooling in DevSecOps are well-positioned to deliver secure, reliable, and innovative software products at an unprecedented pace. It is a transformative journey where technology, security, and collaboration converge, paving the way for a brighter future in software development.

B. Overview of Popular Security Tools and Technologies

As DevSecOps continues to gain momentum, a wide range of security tools and technologies have emerged to support integrating security practices into the software development lifecycle. These tools and technologies are crucial in identifying vulnerabilities, enforcing security policies, and ensuring software applications' overall security and compliance. Here is a detailed overview of some popular security tools and technologies used in DevSecOps:

1. **Static Application Security Testing (SAST):** SAST tools analyze source code, bytecode, or binary code to identify potential security vulnerabilities and coding errors. They perform a static analysis of the application's codebase, providing insights into common security issues like insecure coding practices, injection attacks, and configurations. Popular SAST tools include SonarQube, Checkmarx, and Fortify.

2. **Dynamic Application Security Testing (DAST):** DAST tools evaluate web application security by simulating real-world attacks. These tools scan web applications for vulnerabilities like cross-site scripting (XSS), SQL injection, and insecure direct object references. They help identify vulnerabilities that may arise due to runtime behaviors or configurations. Popular DAST tools include OWASP ZAP, Burp Suite, and Netsparker.

3. **Interactive Application Security Testing (IAST):** IAST tools combine aspects of both SAST and DAST approaches. They analyze the application during runtime and provide feedback on security vulnerabilities, offering real-time insights into code execution and application behavior. IAST tools can provide highly accurate results with reduced false positives. Examples of IAST tools include Contrast Security, Seeker, and WhiteHat Security.

4. **Software Composition Analysis (SCA):** SCA tools focus on identifying security vulnerabilities and open-source components with known vulnerabilities within an application's software supply chain. These tools scan application dependencies, libraries, and frameworks to highlight vulnerabilities and provide actionable recommendations for remediation. Popular SCA tools include Black Duck, Snyk, and Nexus Lifecycle.

5. **Container Security:** Container security tools address security challenges specific to containerized environments. They focus on vulnerability scanning, image integrity, runtime protection, and secure orchestration of containers. These tools help ensure that containers are secure, compliant, and free from vulnerabilities. Popular container security tools include Anchore, Sysdig Secure, and Aqua Security.

6. **Infrastructure as Code (IaC) Security:** IaC security tools assess the security of infrastructure provisioning and deployment scripts, such as those written in tools like Terraform, CloudFormation, or Ansible. They scan IaC templates and configurations for security misconfigurations, insecure permissions, and potential vulnerabilities. Popular IaC security tools include Checkov, Bridgecrew, and Prowler.

7. **Security Orchestration, Automation, and Response (SOAR):** SOAR platforms enable organizations to streamline and automate security incident response processes. They integrate with various security tools, aggregate alerts, and orchestrate automated responses to security incidents. SOAR platforms help reduce response times, improve efficiency, and ensure consistent incident management practices. Popular SOAR platforms include Demisto (now part of Palo Alto Networks), Splunk Phantom, and IBM Resilient.

8. **Security Information and Event Management (SIEM):** SIEM tools collect, aggregate, and analyze security event logs from various sources within an IT infrastructure. They provide real-time threat detection, incident response, and compliance reporting capabilities. SIEM platforms are crucial in monitoring and correlating security events to identify potential threats. Popular SIEM tools include Splunk Enterprise Security, IBM QRadar, and Elastic SIEM.

9. **Security Testing Automation:** Security testing automation tools encompass various tools and frameworks for automating security testing activities. These tools include frameworks for security unit testing, vulnerability scanning, fuzz testing, and security test automation. Popular security testing automation tools include OWASP Security Shepherd, OWASP WebGoat, and Gauntlt.

10. **Continuous Integration/Continuous Delivery (CI/CD) Security:** CI/CD security tools focus on integrating security practices into the CI/CD pipeline. They enable automated security checks, policy enforcement, and vulnerability scanning at each pipeline stage. CI/CD security tools help ensure that only secure and compliant code is deployed to production. Examples include GitLab CI/CD, Jenkins, and CircleCI, with security plugins and integrations.

The DevSecOps landscape continues to evolve, and new tools and technologies regularly emerge to address the evolving security challenges in software development.

Table 10 **Fortify and Flourish:** Mastering Container Security

Note: Only a few real-world examples are provided for illustrative purposes.

	Best Practices	Potential Dangers	Real-World Example
Container Image Hardening	Implement security measures to harden container images, including minimizing the attack surface, using lightweight base images, and removing unnecessary dependencies.	Using vulnerable or outdated container images can introduce security vulnerabilities into the environment.	Utilize Docker's official images or create custom images based on minimal and secure base images, such as Alpine Linux or Distroless, and regularly update them to address security vulnerabilities.
Image Vulnerability Scanning	Perform regular vulnerability scanning of container images to identify and remediate security vulnerabilities present in the image and its dependencies.	Running containers with known vulnerabilities can expose the system to attacks and compromise the entire container environment.	Integration of vulnerability scanning tools like Clair, Trivy, or Anchore into the CI/CD pipeline to automatically scan container images for vulnerabilities and ensure only images with a clean bill of health are deployed.
Secure Image Registry	Implement proper access controls, authentication, and encryption for the container image registry to ensure the integrity and confidentiality of container images.	Unauthorized access to the image registry can result in tampering with images, unauthorized deployment, or exposure of sensitive information.	Using secure container registries like Docker Trusted Registry, Harbor, or Google Container Registry and enabling features like role-based access control (RBAC), image signing, and encrypted communication.
Container Runtime Protection	Employ runtime security measures to detect and prevent malicious activities within running containers, such as isolating containers, monitoring for abnormal behavior,	Containers with inadequate runtime security controls can be exploited, leading to data breaches, privilege escalation, or lateral movement within the	Utilizing container runtime security tools like Falco, Aqua Security, or Sysdig to monitor container activities, detect anomalies, and enforce runtime policies based on predefined security rules.

	and using runtime protection tools.	container environment.	
Secrets Management	Implement secure methods for managing sensitive information within containers, such as API keys, database credentials, or encryption keys, using secrets management solutions.	Inadequate secrets management can result in unauthorized access to sensitive data, compromising the confidentiality and integrity of the system.	Utilize secrets management tools like HashiCorp Vault, AWS Secrets Manager, or Azure Key Vault to store, retrieve, and manage secrets securely within containers with proper access controls and encryption.
Network Segmentation	Implement network segmentation to isolate containers and control traffic flow, limiting the attack surface and minimizing the potential impact of a container compromise.	A lack of network segmentation can enable lateral movement and allow attackers to access critical resources within the container environment.	Utilizing network policies and tools like Kubernetes Network Policies or Istio to enforce network segmentation, restrict inter-container communication, and control ingress/egress traffic between containers.
Regular Patching and Updates	Keep container hosts and underlying software components up to date with security patches and updates to mitigate known vulnerabilities and maintain a secure environment.	Delayed or neglected patching can leave container hosts and dependencies susceptible to exploitation and compromise.	Implement a patch management process that regularly updates the container host OS, container runtime, and dependencies and utilizes automation tools like Kubernetes rolling updates to ensure minimal downtime during updates.
Container Image Hardening	Implement security measures to harden container images, including minimizing the attack surface, using lightweight base images, and removing unnecessary dependencies.	Using vulnerable or outdated container images can introduce security vulnerabilities into the environment.	Utilize Docker's official images or create custom images based on minimal and secure base images, such as Alpine Linux or Distroless. Regularly update the images to address security vulnerabilities. Remove unnecessary packages and libraries from the image to minimize the attack surface. Implement a

			container image scanning process to ensure the image's integrity.
Image Vulnerability Scanning	Perform regular vulnerability scanning of container images to identify and remediate security vulnerabilities present in the image and its dependencies.	Running containers with known vulnerabilities can expose the system to attacks and compromise the entire container environment.	Integrate vulnerability scanning tools like Clair, Trivy, or Anchore into the CI/CD pipeline. Scan container images during the build process and set up automated scanning as part of the continuous integration process. Ensure vulnerabilities are promptly remediated by updating the base image or applying patches to the affected components.
Secure Image Registry	Implement proper access controls, authentication, and encryption for the container image registry to ensure the integrity and confidentiality of container images.	Unauthorized access to the image registry can result in tampering with images, unauthorized deployment, or exposure of sensitive information.	Utilize secure container registries like Docker Trusted Registry, Harbor, or Google Container Registry. Enable authentication mechanisms, such as token-based access, and enforce role-based access control (RBAC) to restrict access to authorized users—Encrypt communication between the registry and the container hosts to protect against eavesdropping.
Container Runtime Protection	Employ runtime security measures to detect and prevent malicious activities within running containers, such as isolating containers, monitoring for abnormal behavior, and using runtime protection tools.	Containers with inadequate runtime security controls can be exploited, leading to data breaches, privilege escalation, or lateral movement within the container environment.	Implement container isolation mechanisms, such as container sandboxing or runtime constraints, using gVisor or Kata Containers. Utilize runtime security tools like Falco, Aqua Security, or Sysdig to monitor container activities, detect anomalies, and enforce runtime policies based on predefined security rules.

Mastering Container Security

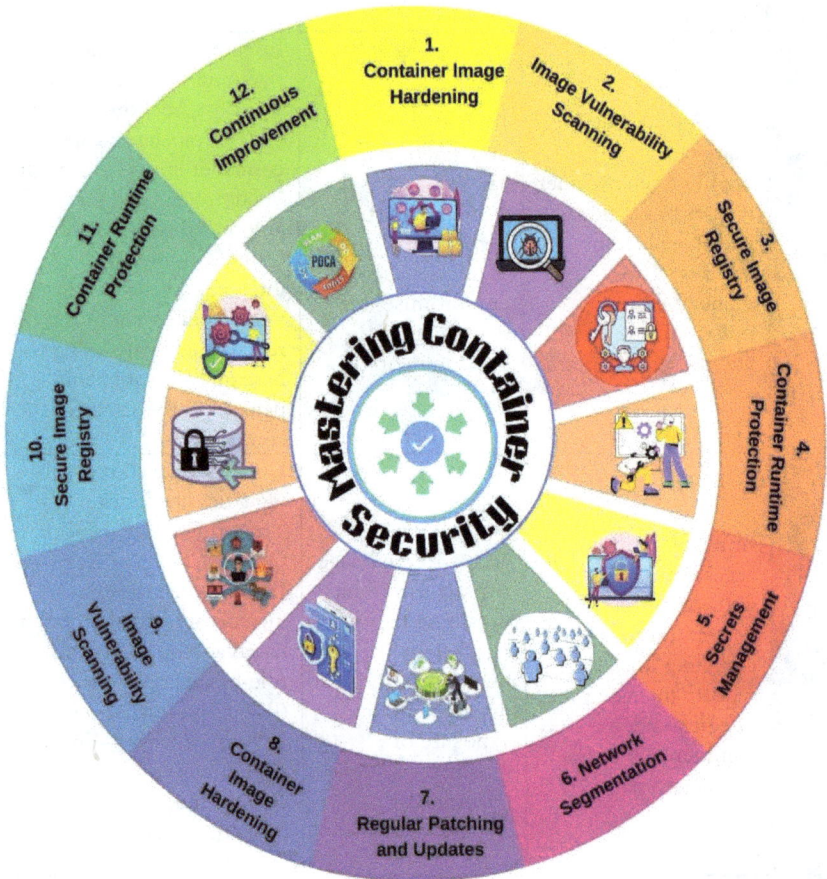

C. Integration of Security Testing Tools into the Pipeline

Integrating security testing tools into the CI/CD pipeline enables automated security checks at each stage. Tools can be triggered to scan code, dependencies, and container images for vulnerabilities and security issues. By integrating security testing as part of the automated pipeline, organizations can identify and remediate security flaws early, ensuring secure software delivery.

As DevSecOps continues to gain momentum, a wide range of security tools and technologies have emerged to support integrating security practices into the software development lifecycle. These tools and technologies are crucial in identifying vulnerabilities, enforcing security policies, and ensuring software applications' overall security and compliance.

D. Use of Automation for Security Policy Enforcement

Automation is vital in enforcing security policies and maintaining a robust security posture within organizations. By leveraging automation tools and technologies, organizations can streamline and strengthen their security policy enforcement processes, saving time and lowering the risk of human oversight.

Automation enables organizations to consistently and efficiently enforce security policies across their entire infrastructure, applications, and systems. With automated tools, security policies can be defined, implemented, and monitored consistently throughout the organization, ensuring compliance with industry policies and internal security standards.

One of the key benefits of automation in security policy enforcement is the ability to achieve real-time and continuous monitoring. Automated tools can monitor system configurations, network traffic, and user activities to detect deviations from established security policies. Any violations or suspicious activities can be flagged and reported immediately, allowing for prompt investigation and remediation.

Organizations can significantly reduce the manual effort required to detect and react to security incidents by automating security policy enforcement. Automated systems can rapidly analyze vast amounts of data, identify security policy violations, and trigger appropriate actions or alerts. This reduces the time and effort spent on manual reviews, freeing security personnel to focus on more complex security tasks.

Automation also facilitates the implementation of proactive security measures. With automated vulnerability scanning, patch management, and configuration management, organizations can promptly identify and remediate vulnerabilities or misconfigurations. This proactive approach minimizes the window of opportunity for potential attackers and enhances the overall security posture.

Moreover, automation helps organizations achieve consistency and standardization in security policy enforcement. Manual procedures are prone to errors and inconsistencies, whereas automation ensures that security policies are applied uniformly across all systems and environments. This reduces the risk of misconfigurations or policy gaps that malicious actors could exploit.

While automation brings numerous advantages, ensuring proper governance and oversight is essential. Regular audits and assessments should be conducted to verify that automated security policy enforcement is aligned with evolving threats and compliance requirements. Security teams must stay updated with emerging technologies and best practices to effectively leverage automation for security policy enforcement.

E. Securing the Code Journey: Policy as Code in CI/CD Pipelines

Policy-as-Code (PaC) is a concept that involves defining and enforcing policies in the form of code in the context of a Continuous Integration/Continuous Deployment (CI/CD) pipeline. In CI/CD pipelines, PaC enables organizations to automate policy checks and ensure that the defined policies are consistently enforced throughout the software development and deployment process.

Policy-as-Code (PaC) revolutionizes how organizations enforce policies governing their operations, processes, and management. Traditionally, policies were documented in static manuals or spreadsheets, leading to challenges in tracking changes and ensuring compliance. PaC transforms policies into executable code using Python, Ruby, JSON, or YAML. These policy scripts contain conditions, constraints, and rules that can be directly executed on infrastructure and applications. Stored in version control systems like Git, the code is processed by policy engines such as Open Policy Agent, CASL, or Sentinel, enabling automated decisions based on policy logic. By integrating PaC within development pipelines, developers can code, review, and test policies alongside application code, ensuring clarity, auditability, and adherence to policy requirements.

The CI/CD pipeline sequence of automated steps permits developers to build, test, and deploy their code rapidly and reliably to production environments. It typically includes stages like code compilation, unit testing, integration testing, containerization, and deployment. Policy-as-Code integrates policy enforcement into this pipeline, ensuring the software adheres to specific standards, regulations, or best practices before it reaches production.

E.1 - Empower Your CI/CD Journey with Policy-as-Code: Automate Compliance, Supercharge Security

Here are some critical points about Policy-as-Code in CI/CD pipelines:

- **Policy Definition:** Policies are rules, guidelines, or constraints the software must meet to ensure compliance, security, quality, or any other specific requirements. These policies can be related to code quality, security practices, architectural guidelines, or different compliance standards.

- **Representation as Code**: Instead of defining policies in separate documentation or manually checking them, Policy-as-Code represents policies as code. This code is written in a domain-specific or general-purpose programming language that humans and machines can understand.

- **Automated Checks**: Within the CI/CD pipeline, tools are integrated to evaluate the code against the defined policies automatically. This automation enables quick and reliable policy enforcement without manual intervention.

- **Early Feedback and Fast Iteration**: By integrating PaC into the CI/CD pipeline, developers receive early feedback on policy violations, allowing them to fix issues quickly and iterate their code more efficiently.

- **Consistency and Standardization**: Policy-as-Code ensures that all software deployments adhere to the same policies, promoting consistency and standardization across the development and deployment processes.

- **Auditing and Compliance**: PaC helps with auditing and compliance efforts since all policy checks and their outcomes are logged and easily accessible. This traceability is crucial for meeting regulatory requirements and adhering to specific standards.

- **Policy as Part of Codebase**: Policies defined as code become part of the project's codebase and version control system. This makes it easier for teams to collaborate on and manage policy definitions throughout the software development lifecycle.

♦ **Policy-as-Code in CI/CD** pipelines is a powerful approach to enforcing governance, improving security, and maintaining code quality in an automated and scalable manner. It allows the teams to achieve higher confidence in their software deployments while maintaining agility and developer productivity.

E.2 - Building Digital Foundations vs. Securing Digital Boundaries: Unveiling the Distinction between IaC and PaC.

Infrastructure as Code (IaC) and Policy as Code (PaC) are concepts associated with managing and automating various aspects of an organization's IT infrastructure and operations.

Infrastructure as Code focuses on automating and managing infrastructure provisioning and configuration, while Policy as Code focuses on automating and enforcing policies, security controls, and compliance requirements.

These approaches help organizations achieve a more efficient, consistent, secure infrastructure and operational environment. By leveraging IaC and PaC, teams can improve collaboration, reduce errors, and increase their systems' overall reliability and security.

Let's explore each of them in detail and examine some Use Cases:

1. **Infrastructure as Code (IaC):**
   Infrastructure as Code is an approach to managing and provisioning infrastructure using machine-readable definition files instead of traditional manual processes. The core idea behind IaC is to treat infrastructure configurations, such as servers, networks, and storage, as Code, which can be versioned, tested, and deployed just like application code. This approach brings several benefits:

Benefits	Description
Consistency and Reproducibility	By representing infrastructure as Code, you can ensure the environments are consistent across development, testing, and production stages, eliminating configuration drift and potential issues caused by manual setups.
Version Control	Infrastructure code can be stored in version control systems like Git, allowing teams to track changes, collaborate effectively, and revert to previous working configurations if needed.
Automated Provisioning	Using tools like Terraform or CloudFormation, you can automatically provision and manage cloud resources or on-premises infrastructure, reducing manual errors and saving time.
Documentation and Visibility	The infrastructure code serves as documentation for the environment, making it easier for new team members to understand the setup and make the infrastructure more transparent.
Scalability	With IaC, scaling your infrastructure becomes more manageable since you can programmatically define how to create additional resources as demand increases.

2. **Policy as Code (PaC):**

    Policy as Code is an approach to enforcing and managing organizational policies, security controls, and compliance requirements through machine-readable policy definitions. Instead of relying solely on human interpretation and manual checks, PaC allows organizations to codify policies, making them machine-executable and auditable. This approach brings several advantages:

Benefits	Description
Consistency and Compliance	By defining policies as Code, you can ensure uniform application of rules and policies across your infrastructure, applications, and operations, reducing the risk of non-compliance.
Automated Compliance Checking	PaC tools can automatically assess whether your infrastructure and applications meet the defined policies, allowing for continuous monitoring and immediate feedback on policy violations.

Integration into CI/CD Pipelines	Policy checks can be included in the continuous integration and continuous deployment (CI/CD) pipeline, preventing non-compliant changes from being deployed to production.
Audit Trail and Governance	PaC allows you to keep a detailed audit trail of policy checks and enforcement actions, providing transparency and accountability for compliance efforts.
Agility and Flexibility	As policies are defined as Code, they can be versioned, updated, and modified in response to changing requirements and regulations.

Table 11 Best practices for implementing **Policy-as-Code (PaC)**

By adopting these best practices for implementing Policy-as-Code, organizations can maximize the benefits of policy automation, enhance security and compliance, and streamline the development and deployment processes.

Practice	Description
Define Clear Policy Goals:	Identify the policy goals you want to achieve with PaC. Clear objectives, whether security, compliance, cost optimization, or code quality, will guide your implementation.
Involve Stakeholders Early	Engage developers, security teams, compliance officers, and other stakeholders from the beginning to gather diverse perspectives and ensure buy-in for PaC adoption.
Use a Policy-as-Code Language	Select a policy language that is easy to read, understand, and maintain. Common choices include Rego (used with Open Policy Agent), JSON, YAML, or domain-specific languages tailored to your organization's needs.
Version Control Policies	Store PaC scripts in version control (e.g., Git) to track changes, review history, and collaborate efficiently. This ensures transparency and enables reverting to previous versions if needed.
Continuous Integration of Policies	Integrate PaC checks into your CI/CD pipelines to assess policy compliance during development and deployment. This promotes early feedback and helps catch policy violations before they reach production.

Automated Testing of Policies	Create automated tests for your PaC scripts to validate their correctness. This ensures that policies function as expected and provides confidence in their enforcement.
Policy as Code Reviews	Treat PaC scripts like any other code and conduct thorough code reviews. Involve subject matter experts and domain specialists to ensure the policies are well-designed and aligned with the organization's goals.
Granular Policy Definitions	Break down complex policies into smaller, modular components for easier maintenance and reusability. This approach helps manage policies across multiple projects and environments efficiently.
Document Policy Intentions	Provide clear documentation for each policy to explain its purpose, reasoning, and impact on the system. This aids in understanding policy decisions and eases communication with stakeholders.
Role-Based Access Control for Policies	Implement role-based access control (RBAC) for PaC scripts to limit modifications and ensure only authorized individuals can manage and update policies.
Policy Lifecycle Management	Establish a process for reviewing, updating, and retiring policies as the organization's needs evolve. Regularly assess policies to ensure they remain relevant and practical.
Policy Testing in Staging Environment	Test policies initially in the staging environment before deploying them to production to verify their impact and reduce the risk of unexpected consequences.
Policy Violation Alerts	Configure alerts and notifications for policy violations. This ensures that the relevant teams are promptly notified of potential security or compliance issues.
Auditing and Logging	Implement auditing and logging mechanisms to record policy evaluations and decisions. This helps with compliance reporting and post-incident analysis.
Continuous Learning and Improvement	Continuously monitor and analyze the effectiveness of policies. Collect feedback from developers and stakeholders to refine and optimize policies over time.
Adopt Industry Standards and Frameworks	Leverage established security frameworks (e.g., CIS Benchmarks) and best practices to ensure comprehensive policy coverage.

Consider Human Readability	While policy scripts are designed for automation, they prioritize human readability and maintainability to ease collaboration and comprehension.
Training and Skill Development	Provide training and resources for teams to become proficient in writing, reviewing, and understanding PaC scripts. Encourage skill development and knowledge sharing.
Cloud-Native Policy Integration	If operating in cloud environments, leverage cloud-native tools for policy enforcement and integration with your cloud provider's services (e.g., AWS Config, Azure Policy).
Continuous Feedback Loop	Foster a culture of continuous feedback and improvement. Encourage developers and teams to provide policy feedback and advocate for a collaborative approach to PaC.

Table 12 **Unleashing the Power of PaC:** Turbocharge Your CI/CD Pipeline with Automated Policy Enforcement-Use Cases

Discover the transformative capabilities of Policy-as-Code (PaC) as it revolutionizes the Continuous Integration/Continuous Deployment (CI/CD) pipeline, automating policy enforcement and elevating security, compliance, and development practices. With its robust and flexible approach, PaC applies seamlessly to diverse use cases, ensuring consistency and safeguarding software integrity throughout the software development and deployment lifecycle. Let's explore how PaC empowers organizations to achieve unparalleled efficiency and confidence in their development processes.

	Use Case	Application
	Container Registry Security	
1	Container Image Scanning and Vulnerability Checks Description	In a CI/CD pipeline, PaC can enforce policies that mandate scanning container images for vulnerabilities before they are pushed to the container registry. PaC scripts can integrate with image scanning tools to automatically check for known security issues, ensuring that only secure images are deployed to production.
2	Registry Access Control Policies Description	PaC can enforce access control policies on container registries to restrict who can push or pull images. By integrating PaC into the CI/CD pipeline, developers must adhere to specific access permissions, lowering the risk of unauthorized admission or distribution of sensitive images.

Code Quality and Best Practices		
1	Code Linting and Formatting Description	PaC can enforce code linting and formatting policies as part of the CI/CD process. PaC scripts can run code analysis tools to check for syntax errors, coding standards, and code style. This helps maintain a consistent codebase and improves the overall quality of the software.
2	Test Coverage Requirements Description	PaC can enforce policies that mandate minimum test coverage before code can be combined into the main branch. PaC scripts can analyze test reports to ensure that new features and bug fixes are adequately tested, reducing the likelihood of regression issues.
Infrastructure as Code (IaC) Governance:		
1	Cloud Resource Tagging Policies Description	In a CI/CD pipeline, PaC can enforce policies that require all cloud resources to be appropriately tagged. PaC scripts can validate the presence of required tags, ensuring proper resource categorization and easy cost allocation and management.
2	Cloud Service IAM Roles and Permissions Description	PaC can enforce policies restricting the permissions granted to cloud services and IAM (Identity and Access Management) roles. PaC scripts can verify that services and roles have the least privilege necessary, reducing the attack surface and potential security risks.
Security Compliance and Auditing		
1	Use Case: Security Configuration Checks Description	PaC can be used to enforce policies that check for security misconfigurations in cloud services or server configurations. PaC scripts can validate security settings against industry best practices and benchmarks, ensuring a secure infrastructure.
2	Compliance Reporting and Documentation Description	PaC can assist in generating compliance reports and documentation as part of the CI/CD process. PaC scripts can automatically generate audit logs, security reports, and compliance documentation, reducing the manual effort required for compliance reporting.
Deployment Approval and Promotion Policies		
1	Multi-Environment Deployment Control Description	PaC can enforce policies that dictate the approval process for deploying code to different environments (e.g., development, staging, production). PaC scripts can check for approvals and conditions before promoting code to the following environment.

2	Approval Gates for Production Deployment Description	PaC can enforce policies that require specific approval gates before deploying code to production. PaC scripts can check for code reviews, successful tests, and other prerequisites, ensuring that critical steps are not skipped in the deployment process.
	Secrets Management and Access Control	
1	Secure Handling of CI/CD Pipeline Secrets Description	PaC can enforce policies to ensure that CI/CD pipeline secrets (e.g., API keys and passwords) are handled securely. PaC scripts can check for encryption, usage restrictions, and access controls on secrets, reducing the risk of unauthorized access to sensitive information.
2	Secret Rotation Policies Description	PaC can enforce policies that mandate regular CI/CD pipeline secret rotation. PaC scripts can check for the last rotation date and trigger alerts when secrets are due for rotation, enhancing the security of the development process.
	Dependency Vulnerability Scanning	
1	Third-Party Dependency Checks Description	PaC can enforce policies that require scanning third-party dependencies for known vulnerabilities. PaC scripts can integrate with dependency scanning tools to check for security issues, ensuring that the project uses the latest and most secure versions of libraries.
2	Blocking Vulnerable Dependencies Description	PaC can enforce policies to block the use of specific versions of dependencies with known vulnerabilities. PaC scripts can automatically prevent the use of blacklisted dependencies, safeguarding the application against potential exploits.
	Infrastructure Validation and Compliance	
1	Infrastructure Provisioning Policy Checks Description	PaC can enforce policies that validate the correctness of infrastructure provisioning configurations. PaC scripts can verify that infrastructure as code (IaC) templates meet organizational standards and best practices before deployment.
2	Resource Naming Conventions Description	PaC can enforce policies for consistent resource naming conventions across infrastructure components. PaC scripts can check that resources are named according to predefined standards, aiding in an organization and reducing naming conflicts.
	Environment Consistency and Configuration Management	

1	Environment Parity Checks Description	PaC can enforce policies to ensure consistent development, staging, and production environments. PaC scripts can verify that configurations, software versions, and dependencies are aligned across environments, reducing the risk of environment-related issues.
2	Configuration Drift Detection Description	PaC can enforce policies that detect configuration drift in deployed environments. PaC scripts can compare the actual configurations against the desired state, triggering alerts when deviations are detected and enabling prompt corrective actions.
Compliance and Change Management		
1	CI/CD Pipeline Change Approvals Description	PaC can enforce policies that mandate approvals for CI/CD pipeline changes. PaC scripts can check for the appropriate reviews and sign-offs before allowing changes to take effect, enhancing the control and security of the pipeline.
2	Version Control and Audit Trails Description	PaC can enforce policies to maintain version control and audit trails for CI/CD pipeline configurations. PaC scripts can log changes and keep a history of modifications, facilitating traceability and compliance with change management practices.
Deployment Rollback Policies		
1	Rollback on Test Failure Description	PaC can enforce policies that automatically trigger a rollback of a deployment if critical tests fail in a specific environment. PaC scripts can check test results and revert to the previous working version, ensuring the integrity of the deployed application.
2	Rollback on Production Monitoring Anomalies Description	PaC can enforce policies that monitor production application metrics and automatically trigger a rollback if anomalies or abnormal behavior are detected. PaC scripts can integrate with monitoring tools and initiate rollbacks to maintain the stability of the production environment.
License Compliance		
1	Open Source License Verification Description	PaC can enforce policies that verify the usage of open-source components in the project and check for license compatibility. PaC scripts can scan dependencies for license information and alert developers about potential licensing issues.

2	Blocking Restricted Licenses Description	PaC can enforce policies that block specific restricted licenses or enforce a safelist of approved licenses. PaC scripts can prevent the accidental inclusion of non-compliant licenses, reducing legal and compliance risks.
Infrastructure Cost Optimization		
1	Resource Cost Management Description	PaC can enforce policies that monitor cloud resource usage and spending. PaC scripts can check for idle or underutilized resources and trigger alerts or automatic scaling to optimize costs.
2	Preventing Costly Actions Description	PaC can enforce policies to prevent specific costly actions, such as resizing expensive instances or provisioning high-cost resources without proper approvals. PaC scripts can ensure that only authorized users can initiate such actions.
Performance and Scalability Checks		
1	Performance Baseline Verification Description	PaC can enforce policies that compare the performance of newly deployed versions against a performance baseline. PaC scripts can check for significant response times or resource utilization deviations, helping maintain application performance.
2	Auto-Scaling Policies Description	PaC can enforce policies that automatically adjust the number of application instances based on real-time metrics (e.g., CPU utilization, network traffic). PaC scripts can facilitate auto-scaling to handle increased demand and maintain service availability.
Disaster Recovery and High Availability		
1	Disaster Recovery (DR) Environment Validation Description	PaC can enforce policies that validate the readiness of the DR environment. PaC scripts can check for synchronization between primary and DR environments and trigger alerts if the DR environment is not current.
2	High Availability (HA) Configuration Checks Description	PaC can enforce policies that verify the configuration of a high-availability setup. PaC scripts can ensure that load balancers, failover mechanisms, and redundant components are correctly configured to maintain continuous service availability.

Incorporating Policy-as-Code (PaC) into the CI/CD pipeline is a strategic move that empowers organizations to seamlessly integrate policy enforcement into their software development and deployment workflows. This integration results in elevated security and compliance levels and drives a more efficient and dependable CI/CD process, ultimately accelerating the delivery of high-quality software. Implementing specific use cases of PaC within the CI/CD pipeline further enhances security, enforces best practices, maintains compliance, and ensures consistency throughout the entire software development and deployment lifecycle. PaC becomes an integral and indispensable part of the development workflow, providing automated checks and ensuring policies are consistently enforced reliably and efficiently. By leveraging these CI/CD pipeline-specific examples of Policy-as-Code, organizations can significantly enhance the reliability, security, and efficiency of their development and deployment processes, positioning PaC as a crucial tool for automating checks, promoting best practices, and ensuring unwavering adherence to critical policies throughout the CI/CD pipeline.

Table 13 Unlocking Success: The Power of Policy-as-Code (PaC) in Streamlined Development and Deployment

Policy-as-Code enhances the software development lifecycle by automating policy checks, fostering collaboration, and ensuring a robust and secure deployment process. It empowers organizations to deliver high-quality software faster while meeting regulatory requirements and industry best procedures. Here are some aspects to keep in mind.

1.	**Automated Policy Enforcement**: PaC defines policies as code, enabling automatic checks and enforcement throughout the CI/CD pipeline. This automation ensures that policies are consistently applied, lowering the risk of human oversight and improving security and compliance.
2.	**Version Control and Auditing**: Storing policies as code in version control systems like Git enables easy tracking of changes over time. This versioning facilitates auditing and compliance efforts, providing a clear history of policy updates and their impact on the software.
3.	**Continuous Compliance**: With PaC integrated into the development process, compliance becomes a continuous and seamless part of the workflow. Developers receive instant feedback on policy violations, enabling them to address issues early in the development cycle.
4.	**Improved Collaboration**: Policy code becomes part of the application's codebase, promoting collaboration between developers, security teams, and other stakeholders. This shared understanding of policies fosters alignment and ensures that policy updates are communicated effectively.

5.	**Faster Iterations and Deployment**: By automating policy checks, developers can quickly iterate on their code and confidently deploy changes. PaC reduces manual approval processes, streamlining development and accelerating software delivery.
6.	**Consistency and Standardization**: PaC enforces policies consistently across all deployments, leading to standardized practices and reducing configuration drift. This consistency enhances the overall stability and reliability of the application.
7.	**Increased Security and Risk Mitigation**: Automated policy enforcement reduces the likelihood of security vulnerabilities and other risks. PaC can check for weak passwords, validate code quality, and enforce access controls, bolstering the application's security posture.
8.	**Transparency and Traceability**: Policy code is transparent and accessible, providing insights into the rules and constraints applied to the software. The traceability of policy decisions helps troubleshoot and understand the reasoning behind specific actions.
9.	**Scalability and Reusability**: PaC allows policies to be written as reusable code modules, simplifying applying consistent policies across multiple projects and environments. This scalability is essential for large and complex development ecosystems.
10.	**Alignment with DevSecOps Culture**: PaC aligns with the principles of DevSecOps by integrating policy enforcement into the development process. It promotes a culture of shared responsibility, where developers actively ensure compliance and security.

Policy as Code (PaC)Best Practice Assessment

Policy as code (PaC) is a modern approach to managing and enforcing policies within an organization's IT infrastructure and software development processes. It blends the principles of DevSecOps, automation, and compliance by treating policies as code and representing and managing policies using code and automation tools.

Practice	Description	Practice	Description
Define Clear Policy Goals	Identify the policy goals you want to achieve with PaC. Clear objectives, whether security, compliance, cost optimization, or code quality, will guide your implementation.	Policy Lifecycle Management	Establish a process for reviewing, updating, and retiring policies as the organization's needs evolve. Regularly assess policies to ensure they remain relevant and practical.
Involve Stakeholders Early	Engage developers, security teams, compliance officers, and other stakeholders from the beginning to gather diverse perspectives and ensure buy-in for PaC adoption.	Policy Testing in Staging Environment	Test policies initially in the staging environment before deploying them to production to verify their impact and reduce the risk of unexpected consequences.
Use a Policy-as-Code Language	Select a policy language that is easy to read, understand, and maintain. Common choices include Rego (used with Open Policy Agent), JSON, YAML, or domain-specific languages tailored to your organization's needs.	Policy Violation Alerts	Configure alerts and notifications for policy violations. This ensures that the relevant teams are promptly notified of potential security or compliance issues.
Version Control Policies	Store PaC scripts in version control (e.g., Git) to track changes, review history, and collaborate efficiently. This ensures transparency and enables reverting to previous versions if needed.	Auditing and Logging	Implement auditing and logging mechanisms to record policy evaluations and decisions. This helps with compliance reporting and post-incident analysis.
Continuous Integration of Policies	Integrate PaC checks into your CI/CD pipelines to automatically assess policy compliance during the development and deployment process. This promotes early feedback and helps catch policy violations before they reach production	Continuous Learning and Improvement	Continuously monitor and analyze the effectiveness of policies. Collect feedback from developers and stakeholders to refine and optimize policies over time.
Automated Testing of Policies	Create automated tests for your PaC scripts to validate their correctness. This ensures that policies function as expected and provides confidence in their enforcement.	Adopt Industry Standards and Frameworks	Leverage established security frameworks (e.g., CIS Benchmarks) and best practices to ensure comprehensive policy coverage.
Policy as Code Reviews	Treat PaC scripts like any other code and conduct thorough code reviews. Involve subject matter experts and domain specialists to ensure the policies are well-designed and aligned with the organization's goals.	Consider Human Readability	While policy scripts are designed for automation, prioritize human readability and maintainability to ease collaboration and comprehension.
Granular Policy Definitions	Break down complex policies into smaller, modular components for easier maintenance and reusability. This approach helps manage policies across multiple projects and environments efficiently.	Training and Skill Development	Provide training and resources for teams to become proficient in writing, reviewing, and understanding PaC scripts. Encourage skill development and knowledge sharing.
Document Policy Intentions	Provide clear documentation for each policy to explain its purpose, reasoning, and impact on the system. This aids in understanding policy decisions and eases communication with stakeholders.	Cloud-Native Policy Integration	If operating in cloud environments, leverage cloud-native tools for policy enforcement and integration with your cloud provider's services (e.g., AWS Config, Azure Policy).
Role-Based Access Control for Policies	Implement role-based access control (RBAC) for PaC scripts to limit modifications and ensure only authorized individuals can manage and update policies.	Continuous Feedback Loop	Foster a culture of continuous feedback and improvement. Encourage developers and teams to provide policy feedback and advocate for a collaborative approach to PaC.

Hands-on tool: Snapshot of Policy as Code Practice Assessment

VI. Securing Containerized Environments

A. Revolutionizing CI/CD: Unleashing the Power of Containerization

Containerization is crucial in the Continuous Integration and Continuous Deployment (CI/CD) pipeline, revolutionizing software development and delivery practices. Here's an overview of how containerization fits into the CI/CD pipeline:

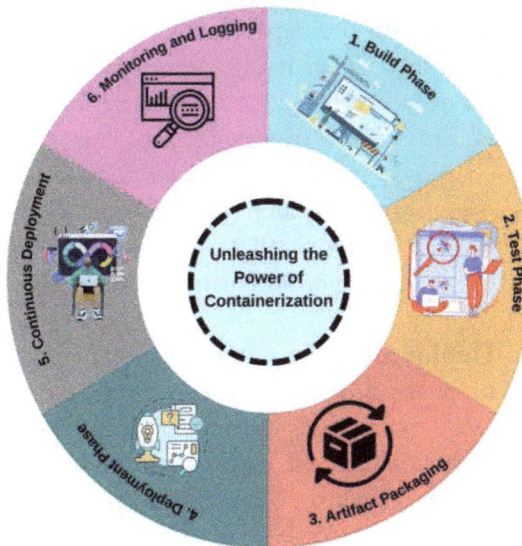

1. **Build Phase:** In the CI/CD pipeline build phase, developers commit code changes to a version control system (e.g., Git). Continuous-integration tools like Jenkins or GitLab CI/CD monitor the repository for changes. When changes are detected, the CI tool initiates a build process. Containers create reproducible build environments by encapsulating the application code, dependencies, and build tools.

2. **Test Phase:** Once the build phase is complete, the CI/CD pipeline moves to the testing phase. Containers are employed to provide

consistent and isolated testing environments. Automated tests, including unit, integration, and end-to-end tests, are executed within containers. Containers ensure that the test environment is identical to the production environment, helping to catch potential issues early in the development process.

3. **Artifact Packaging:** After successful testing, the CI/CD pipeline packages the application artifacts, including binaries, libraries, and configuration files, into a container image. The container image contains the entire runtime environment needed to run the application. This image is a portable and immutable artifact that can be clearly deployed to various environments.

4. **Deployment Phase:** In the deployment phase, the container image is pushed to a container registry, such as Docker Hub or Amazon ECR, which serves as a centralized repository for container images. The deployment process retrieves the container image from the registry and deploys it to the target environment, such as development, staging, or production. Container orchestration tools like Kubernetes are often used to manage the deployment of containerized applications across clusters of machines.

5. **Continuous Deployment:** In a continuous deployment scenario, the deployment phase is automated triggered by a successful build and test process. Containers allow for seamless and consistent deployment of applications across different environments, reducing the risk of deployment failures or environment inconsistencies.

6. **Monitoring and Logging:** Containers enable the collection of metrics and logs from running applications. Monitoring tools can be integrated into the CI/CD pipeline to track containerized applications' performance, health, and availability. This data helps identify and resolve issues quickly, improving overall application quality.

Containerization simplifies the CI/CD pipeline by providing lightweight and portable units of deployment that can be consistently tested, packaged, and deployed. It enables faster feedback loops, improves collaboration among development teams, and facilitates the delivery of high-quality software with greater efficiency and reliability.

B. Exploring Dynamic Use Cases for Maximum Efficiency

Containerization has become increasingly popular due to its numerous benefits, including portability, scalability, and resource efficiency. Here are some simple use cases for containerizing workloads:

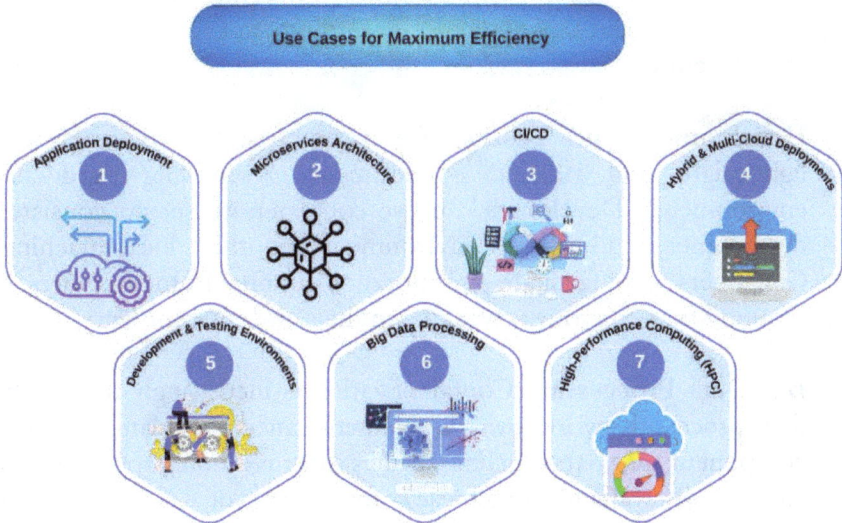

Use Cases for Maximum Efficiency

1. **Application Deployment:** Containerization allows you to package your application and its dependencies and runtime environment into a portable container. This makes it easier to deploy the application consistently across different environments, such as development, testing, and production, without worrying about compatibility issues.

2. **Microservices Architecture:** Containerization is well-suited for building and deploying microservices-based architectures. Each microservice can be containerized, allowing it to run independently and scale horizontally. Containers provide isolation between services, making it easier to manage and update individual components of a complex system.

3. **Continuous Integration and Continuous Deployment (CI/CD):** Containers are crucial to CI/CD pipelines. By containerizing your

application, you can create reproducible build artifacts that can be tested and deployed automatically. Containers enable consistent testing and deployment across different pipeline stages, leading to faster and more reliable software delivery.

4. **Hybrid and Multi-Cloud Deployments:** Containers enable workload portability, allowing you to deploy applications across cloud providers or on-premises environments. This flexibility benefits hybrid and multi-cloud deployments, where you can consistently run containers regardless of the underlying infrastructure.

5. **Development and Testing Environments:** Containers provide lightweight and isolated environments resembling production environments. Developers can use containers to set up consistent development and testing environments on their local machines. Containers also facilitate collaboration among team members by ensuring that everyone is working in the same environment.

6. **Big Data Processing:** Containerization is increasingly used in big data processing workflows. Containers can encapsulate individual components of a data pipeline, such as data ingestion, processing, and analytics. By containerizing these components, you can achieve better resource utilization and faster deployment of data-intensive applications.

7. **High-Performance Computing (HPC):** Containerization is adopted in HPC environments to improve resource utilization and simplify software management. Containers allow researchers and scientists to package their computational workloads with all the required dependencies and libraries, making sharing and reproducing experiments across different HPC clusters easier.

C. Shielding the DevSecOps Realm: Best Practices for Container Security in the CI/CD Pipeline

Containerization has revolutionized software development, enabling organizations to achieve greater agility and efficiency. However, the adoption of containerization also brings new challenges, particularly in ensuring the security of the CI/CD pipeline. This section explores the importance of container security in safeguarding the pipeline and provides a comprehensive set of best practices to mitigate risks effectively.

Container security is critical to building and deploying CI/CD pipeline applications. Containers offer numerous software development and deployment benefits and introduce new security considerations. Ensuring the security of containerized applications throughout the CI/CD pipeline is essential to protect sensitive data, prevent unauthorized access, and mitigate potential vulnerabilities. For a comprehensive overview of container security best practices, please refer to Table 10 Fortify and Flourish: Mastering Container Security.

D. Container Orchestration Platforms for Next-Level Security

Container orchestration platforms like Kubernetes provide powerful tools and features to manage and scale containerized applications. To best utilize container orchestration platforms securely, consider the following practices:

1. **Secure Cluster Configuration:**
   - Implement secure network communication within the cluster using Transport Layer Security (TLS) certificates.
   - Disable or restrict access to the Kubernetes API server to prevent unauthorized access.
   - Enforce robust authentication mechanisms like client certificates or integration with external identity providers.
   - Regularly review and audit cluster configuration to ensure compliance with security best practices.

2. **RBAC and Access Controls:**
   - Utilize Role-Based Access Control (RBAC) to grant appropriate permissions to users and service accounts within the cluster.
   - Follow the principle of least privilege, granting only necessary permissions to individuals or entities.
   - Regularly review and update access controls as roles and responsibilities change.

3. **Secrets Management:**
   - Use Kubernetes Secrets or external management solutions to store and distribute sensitive information securely.
   - Avoid storing secrets directly in container specifications or environment variables.
   - Encrypt and protect secrets at rest and in transit.

4. **Pod Security Policies:**
   - Implement Pod Security Policies (PSPs) to define security constraints for pods within the cluster.
   - Enforce restrictions on privilege escalation, host namespace sharing, container capabilities, and other security-sensitive aspects.

- Regularly review and update PSPs to align with security requirements.

5. **Network Segmentation:**
   - Employ network segmentation to isolate sensitive workloads or namespaces from other cluster parts.
   - Utilize network policies to enforce communication restrictions between pods and namespaces.
   - Implement network-level encryption, such as Virtual Private Networks (VPNs) or secure overlay networks, to protect traffic between nodes and clusters.

6. **Container Image Security:**
   - Regularly scan container images for vulnerabilities and security issues using vulnerability scanning tools.
   - Implement image signing and verification mechanisms to ensure the integrity and authenticity of container images.
   - Enforce image provenance and only allow trusted images to be deployed within the cluster.

7. **Monitoring and Logging:**
   - Implement comprehensive monitoring and logging solutions to capture and analyze cluster activity and security events.
   - Set up alerts and automated responses for security incidents or abnormal behavior.
   - Regularly review logs to identify potential security breaches or anomalous activities.

8. **Regular Updates and Patching:**
   - Stay updated with security patches and updates for the container orchestration platform, including the Kubernetes control plane and worker nodes.
   - Follow the vendor's security announcements and apply patches promptly.
   - Regularly monitor new vulnerabilities and apply mitigations as necessary.

9. **Security Testing and Auditing:**
   - Conduct regular security testing, including vulnerability scanning, penetration testing, and configuration audits.

- Perform periodic security audits to assess the overall security posture of the cluster.
- Implement secure coding practices for applications deployed within the cluster.

10. Education and Training:
- Provide education and training to administrators, developers, and other stakeholders to ensure awareness of security best practices.
- Foster a security-first mindset and encourage a culture of security within the organization.
- Stay informed about emerging security threats and new best practices through industry resources and communities.

By adopting these practices, one can enhance the security of the container orchestration platform and mitigate potential risks associated with managing and scaling containerized applications.

E. Unlocking the Power of Container Orchestration Platforms

Table 14 **Popular container orchestration platforms**

Several container orchestration platforms are available, each offering different features and capabilities. Here are some popular container orchestration platforms:

1	**Kubernetes:** Kubernetes is the most widely adopted container orchestration platform. It provides a strong set of features for deploying, managing, and scaling containerized applications across clusters of machines. Kubernetes offers advanced scheduling, automated scaling, self-healing capabilities, service discovery, and load balancing.	
2	**Docker Swarm**: Docker Swarm is a native clustering and orchestration solution provided by Docker. It allows you to create and manage a cluster of Docker nodes, providing features like service discovery, load balancing, rolling updates, and high availability. Docker Swarm is known for its simplicity and ease of use.	
3	**Amazon Elastic Container Service (ECS):** Amazon ECS is a fully managed container orchestration service provided by Amazon Web Services (AWS). It integrates with other AWS services, such as EC2, IAM, and CloudWatch, and allows you to deploy and scale containerized applications quickly. ECS supports Amazon EC2 instances and AWS Fargate, a serverless container compute engine.	
4	**Google Kubernetes Engine (GKE)**: GKE is a managed Kubernetes service that Google Cloud Platform (GCP) provides. It offers a fully managed Kubernetes control plane and simplifies the deployment and management of containerized applications on GCP. GKE integrates with other GCP services, such as Identity and Access Management (IAM), Stackdriver for logging and monitoring, and Cloud Load Balancing.	

5	**Azure Kubernetes Service (AKS):** AKS is a managed Kubernetes service provided by Microsoft Azure. It enables you to deploy, manage, and scale containerized applications using Kubernetes on Azure. AKS integrates with other Azure services, such as Azure Active Directory (AAD), Azure Monitor for monitoring, and Azure Load Balancer for load balancing.	
	6	**Red Hat OpenShift:** OpenShift is a Kubernetes-based container platform developed by Red Hat. It provides a complete containerization platform with features like automated builds, source-to-image capabilities, developer tools, and enterprise-grade security. OpenShift supports both on-premises and cloud deployments.
7	**HashiCorp Nomad:** Nomad is an open-source workload orchestrator developed by HashiCorp. While not solely focused on containers, Nomad supports containerized applications alongside other workloads, such as VMs and standalone binaries. Nomad provides a flexible and lightweight solution for managing heterogeneous workloads across clusters.	

These are just a few examples of container orchestration platforms available in the market. When choosing a container orchestration platform, consider scalability, ease of use, integration with other tools and services, community support, and compatibility with your existing infrastructure and cloud providers.

Fortify and Flourish: Mastering Container Security and Self Assessment

Project Name: <Enter Project Name>   Assessment Week <Select Week>

G	Fortify and Flourish: Mastering Container Security and Self Assessment	Score Out of 5
	1. Secure Image Creation:	5
	2. Secure Container Configuration:	5
	3. Container Image Security:	5
	4. Container Runtime Security:	5
	5. Container Orchestration Platform Security:	5

Container Security Best Practices : Container security best practices involve implementing various measures to secure containerized environments. Here are some essential best practices with real-world examples:

Hands-on tool: Snapshot of Container Security Assessment

Table 15 **Docker Image Optimization Techniques**

Reducing the size of Docker images is essential for efficient storage and faster deployments. Here are some of the best ways to reduce the size of Docker images:

1.	**Use smaller base images:**	Choose lightweight images like Alpine Linux instead of more significant distributions like Ubuntu. Alpine Linux is known for its small size and security.
2.	**Minimize layers:**	Each instruction in a Dockerfile creates a new layer. Minimizing the number of layers reduces image size. Combine related instructions using RUN statements and clean up unnecessary files and packages in the same layer.
3.	**Remove unnecessary dependencies:**	Review your applications and remove any unnecessary packages or libraries. Only include the required files and dependencies in your Docker image.
4.	**Use multi-stage builds:**	Utilize multi-stage builds to separate the build environment from the final runtime image. Build your application in one stage and copy the necessary artifacts into a minimal base image in the final stage. This way, you can discard unnecessary build tools and dependencies, resulting in a smaller final image.
5.	**Compress and optimize files:**	Compress files before copying them into the Docker image. You can use tools like tar or gzip to reduce file sizes. Optimize images, CSS, and JavaScript files to minimize their size.
6.	**Avoid unnecessary package managers:**	Some package managers, like apt-get in Debian-based images, store package metadata that can increase image size. If possible, use lightweight package managers or package-less distributions.
7.	**Use dockerignore:**	Create a dockerignore file in your project directory to exclude unnecessary files and directories from being copied into the Docker image. This helps avoid including large files or sensitive data not required for the application.
8.	**Clean up after installation:**	Remove temporary files, caches, and package manager metadata after installing dependencies in your Dockerfile. This can be achieved by chaining commands with && or using the RUN instruction with multiple commands.
9.	**Leverage Docker image optimization tools:**	There are tools available that can help optimize Docker images, such as Docker Slim, Squash, or Kaniko. These tools analyze and optimize the image layers to reduce the overall size.
10.	**Consider using alternative runtimes:**	Instead of using a full-fledged runtime like Java or Python, consider using lightweight alternatives like GraalVM or Alpine-based variants, which can result in smaller images.

Table 16 **Docker Demystified:** A Beginner's Journey into Container Magic

Unlock the Magic of Docker for Dummies: Journey into Docker World through Car Design

Stage	Docker Story	Race Car Example
Design Phase	Imagine being a brilliant car designer. You can now create a blueprint (dockerfile) - containing all the specifications and instructions needed to assemble your car/application.	You design the ultimate race car, including the specifications, materials, and components needed to build it.
Build Phase	When you're ready to build your application, using the dockerfile, you run 'docker build.' docker takes the instructions from the dockerfile and creates a unique package. This docker image contains all the required parts and components for your application to run.	With the race car design ready, you start building the actual race car, assembling all the parts and components according to your specifications.
Storage Phase	The docker garage is a massive warehouse where all the ready-to-go application designs (docker images) reside. You can 'park' your application design in this garage or 'bring in' other impressive designs/updated versions created by fellow application designers.	Once the race car is built, you store it in a garage or showroom, along with other exceptional designs from different designers.
Running the Race	To experience the thrill of racing in your specifically designed car (bringing your application version to life), you can use the 'docker run' command, which will spin a container based on your design (image) from the above step, leaving a trail of excitement behind!	With the race car built and ready, you take it to the racetrack and experience the adrenaline rush as you speed through the race, competing with other race cars.
Modificatio n and Upgrades	If you want to make tweaks and improvements to your application design, you use 'docker Commit' to create a new image of your application after making modifications. Alternatively, update the dockerfile with the modifications so that your blueprint is always up to date and follows the instructions from the build phase.	After a thrilling race, you might improve your race car design by adding more horsepower or enhancing aerodynamics.

Sharing the Race Car Experience	You can share your application by distributing the image from your storage location to a broader audience. Alternatively, you can export your container (running application based on a specific image/design) as a tar file with your fellow developers for a quick experience.	If your friends are passionate about race cars, you can share your experience with them by taking them for a ride in your car or providing them with the specifications to build their version.
Retiring the Race Car	When your application has fulfilled its desired outcome, you can make space for newer and faster designs/blueprints by using 'docker rmi' with appropriate options to remove the image from your storage location.	After your race car has served its purpose or is outdated, you may retire it to make way for newer and more advanced race car models.

Docker enables one to design, share, and experience the excitement of innovation, just like building and racing the dream race car!

F. Navigating the DevSecOps Horizon: Empowering CI/CD with Container Orchestration's Vital Role

Container orchestration manages and coordinates containerized applications' deployment, scaling, and operation across a cluster of machines or nodes. It involves automating various tasks related to container management, such as scheduling containers on appropriate nodes, load balancing, networking, service discovery, scaling, and self-healing.

Container orchestration platforms, like Kubernetes, Docker Swarm, and others, provide tools and features to simplify the management of containerized applications at scale. These platforms abstract the complexity of managing individual containers and provide higher-level abstractions, allowing developers and operators to focus on defining the desired state of their applications rather than dealing with low-level infrastructure details.

In the current CI/CD (Continuous Integration/Continuous Deployment) pipeline, container orchestration plays a crucial role. Here's why it is essential:

1. **Scalability and Resource Efficiency:** Container orchestration platforms enable horizontal scaling of applications by automatically distributing containers across multiple nodes. They provide mechanisms for auto-scaling based on metrics or user-defined rules, ensuring the application can efficiently handle increased workload demand.

2. **High Availability and Fault Tolerance**: Container orchestration platforms help ensure the high availability of applications by managing replica sets of containers and automatically rescheduling containers if a node fails. They monitor the health of containers and automatically restart or replace unhealthy instances, improving the application's resiliency.

3. **Infrastructure Abstraction:** Container orchestration platforms abstract away the underlying infrastructure, allowing developers and operators to define and manage applications cloud-agnostic. This enables consistent deployment across different environments, such as development, testing, and production, regardless of the underlying infrastructure provider.

4. **Service Discovery and Load Balancing:** Container orchestration platforms provide built-in service discovery mechanisms, allowing containers to discover and communicate with each other within the cluster easily. They also offer load-balancing features to distribute traffic evenly across containers or services, ensuring optimal performance and resource utilization.

5. **Rolling Updates and Zero Downtime Deployments:** Container orchestration platforms support rolling updates, allowing applications to be updated or patched without downtime. They ensure that a new version of the application is gradually rolled out while the old version is still running, reducing the impact on users and maintaining uninterrupted service.

6. **Infrastructure Automation:** Container orchestration platforms automate many tasks related to infrastructure management, such as provisioning and managing underlying resources, scaling applications, and handling networking and storage. This reduces the operational burden and enables infrastructure automation as part of the CI/CD pipeline.

7. **DevSecOps Collaboration:** Container orchestration platforms promote collaboration between development and operations teams. They provide a standard interface and tooling for both teams to define and manage application deployments, making adopting DevSecOps practices easier and streamlining the CI/CD pipeline.

By leveraging container orchestration platforms in the CI/CD pipeline, organizations can achieve faster and more reliable software delivery, improved scalability and availability, better resource utilization, and simplified infrastructure management. It helps connect the gap between development and operations, enabling seamless integration and automation throughout the software delivery lifecycle.

G. Fortified DevSecOps: A Security-Centric Journey from Source to Deployment

An example of a secure DevSecOps workflow with containers, incorporating security practices at each step of the workflow

1. **Source Code Management:**
   - Developers commit code modifications to a version control system like Git, secured using strong access controls and user authentication.
   - Example: Use GitLab as the source code management platform.

2. **Continuous Integration:**
   - The CI system automatically builds container images from the source code, ensuring proper build and compilation processes.
   - Example: Use Jenkins as the CI tool.

3. **Static Application Security Testing (SAST):**
   - Run static code analysis tools against the source code and container images to identify potential security vulnerabilities.
   - For example, Integrate tools like SonarQube or Snyk for SAST.

4. **Container Image Scanning:**
   - Perform vulnerability scanning on container images to detect and remediate known vulnerabilities or security issues.
   - Example: Utilize tools like Clair or Anchore for image scanning.

5. **Dynamic Application Security Testing (DAST):**
   - Conduct dynamic security testing against containerized applications to identify runtime vulnerabilities and weaknesses.
   - For example, Use tools like OWASP ZAP or Burp Suite for DAST.

6. **Security Compliance and Configuration Auditing:**
   - Regularly audit the container orchestration platform's configuration and compliance with security best practices and industry standards.
   - Example: Employ tools like kube-bench or kube-hunter to assess Kubernetes cluster security.

7. **Secrets Management:**
   - Securely store and manage secrets, such as API keys or database passwords, using a secrets management solution.

- For example, Integrate HashiCorp Vault or Kubernetes Secrets for secrets management.

8. Infrastructure as Code (IaC) Security:
- Apply security practices to the infrastructure provisioning and deployment code, ensuring secure configurations of the container orchestration platform.
- Example: Utilize tools like Terraform or CloudFormation with security-focused configurations.

9. Continuous Monitoring:
- Implement comprehensive logging, monitoring, and alerting solutions to detect and respond to real-time security events or anomalies.
- Example: Employ tools like Prometheus and Grafana for monitoring and ELK Stack (Elasticsearch, Logstash, Kibana) for logging and analysis.

10. Incident Response and Forensics:
- Establish an incident response plan and conduct regular tabletop exercises to ensure the team is prepared to respond to security incidents promptly.
- Example: Define incident response procedures, including steps for containment, analysis, and recovery.

By incorporating these security practices into the DevSecOps workflow, organizations can enhance the security posture of containerized applications, identify vulnerabilities early, and respond to security incidents effectively. Remember that the tools and technologies mentioned are just examples, and choosing the ones that best fit your organization's requirements and preferences is essential.

VII. Collaborating and Educating Development and Security Teams

A. Fostering Collaboration between Development and Security Teams

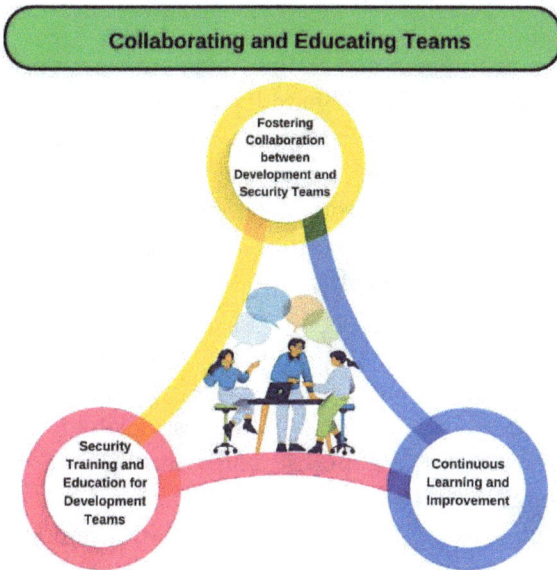

In today's fast-paced and evolving technological landscape, fostering collaboration between development and security teams is essential for building secure and resilient software products. The traditional divide between these teams can lead to siloed approaches and hinder the timely identification and mitigation of security vulnerabilities. By promoting collaboration and establishing effective communication channels, organizations can align their development and security efforts, enhancing the overall security posture of their products and systems.

Collaboration between development and security teams brings several benefits. First and foremost, it enables security considerations to be integrated seamlessly into the software development lifecycle. By involving security experts, developing teams can gain valuable insights and guidance regarding secure coding practices, threat modeling, and vulnerability management. This early involvement reduces the likelihood of security issues being identified late in the development process, minimizing the need for costly rework and ensuring that security is an inherent aspect of the product.

Regular communication and knowledge sharing between development and security teams are crucial for maintaining a shared understanding of security requirements and challenges. This can be achieved through cross-functional meetings, joint training sessions, or establishing dedicated security champions within development teams. Encouraging open dialogue allows for exchanging ideas, identifying potential risks, and collaborative problem-solving. It also helps bridge the gap between security policies and practical implementation, ensuring that security measures are effective and feasible.

Collaborative tools and technologies can further facilitate teamwork between development and security teams. Shared platforms for issue tracking, secure code review, and vulnerability management enable seamless collaboration and efficient resolution of security-related tasks. Integrating security testing and analysis tools into the development workflow ensures that vulnerabilities are identified and addressed early on, promoting a proactive approach to security.

Building a culture of collaboration and mutual respect between development and security teams is crucial for fostering long-term cooperation. This can be achieved by fostering a shared responsibility for security outcomes and recognizing the expertise and contributions of each team. Encouraging joint ownership of security initiatives and celebrating successes as a unified entity promotes a collaborative mindset and fosters a positive working environment.

Lastly, continuous improvement and feedback loops are significant in the collaborative process. Regular retrospective meetings and post-incident reviews allow both teams to reflect on challenges, identify areas for improvement, and refine security practices. By embracing a continuous learning, development, and security culture, teams can adapt and evolve together, effectively addressing emerging threats and evolving security requirements.

B. Security Training and Education for Development Teams

Security training and education are essential for development teams to address the growing cybersecurity threats and build secure software effectively. By providing comprehensive security training, organizations can equip their developers with the knowledge and skills to identify and mitigate security risks, ensuring the development of robust and resilient applications.

One of the primary objectives of security training is to create awareness among development teams about common security vulnerabilities, attack vectors, and secure coding practices. Training programs should cover secure coding techniques, threat modeling, authentication and authorization mechanisms, input validation, and data sanitization. By educating developers about these fundamental security principles, organizations can foster a security-conscious culture and instill a proactive approach to security throughout the development process.

Real-world examples and hands-on exercises should be incorporated into security training programs to provide practical experience and reinforce learning. By simulating real-world scenarios, developers can understand the impact of security vulnerabilities and gain insight into how attackers exploit weaknesses in software systems. Practical exercises, such as secure coding challenges or vulnerability discovery workshops, enhance developers' problem-solving skills and enable them to apply secure coding practices effectively.

In addition to technical aspects, security training should also cover legal and compliance requirements, privacy considerations, and emerging trends in the threat landscape. Developers should know relevant regulations such as GDPR or HIPAA and industry-specific best practices for handling sensitive data. By understanding security's legal and compliance aspects, development groups can ensure that their applications meet the necessary standards and regulations.

Organizations should provide ongoing security education and encourage continuous learning among development teams. The cybersecurity landscape evolves rapidly, with new threats and vulnerabilities emerging regularly. By offering resources such as online courses, workshops, and access to security-focused communities and forums, organizations can empower developers to stay updated on the latest security trends and techniques. Encouraging participation in security conferences and providing opportunities for certifications further enhances the expertise and professionalism of the development team.

To maximize the effectiveness of security training and education, organizations should tailor the programs to the specific needs of their development teams. Consider developers' different skill levels and backgrounds and provide targeted training accordingly. Training programs can also be supplemented with secure coding guidelines, reference materials, and code review processes to ensure consistent adherence to secure coding practices.

C. Continuous Learning and Improvement

In today's dynamic and rapidly evolving technological landscape, continuous learning and improvement are critical for individuals and corporations to stay ahead of the curve and thrive. By adopting a culture of continuous learning, organizations can drive innovation, adapt to changing market demands, and enhance their overall performance and competitiveness.

Continuous learning involves acquiring knowledge, skills, and insights to enhance professional growth and effectiveness. It encompasses various aspects, including staying updated on industry trends, embracing new technologies, and honing existing skills. By encouraging employees to learn continuously, organizations empower their workforce to evolve alongside the ever-changing business environment.

One of the key benefits of constant learning is the ability to adapt and respond to emerging challenges and opportunities. As technologies, methodologies, and market demands evolve, organizations must ensure their workforce is equipped with the latest knowledge and skills. By investing in training programs, workshops, and professional development opportunities, organizations can enable their employees to learn new technologies, industry best practices, and cutting-edge methodologies.

Continuous learning also fosters innovation and creativity within organizations. When staff are encouraged to explore new ideas, experiment with different approaches, and challenge conventional thinking, they are more likely to generate innovative solutions and drive positive change. By creating a supportive environment that encourages curiosity, risk-taking, and knowledge sharing, organizations can nurture a culture of innovation and foster a growth mindset.

Furthermore, continuous learning promotes personal and professional growth among employees. It helps them develop new competencies, expand their skill sets, and enhance their career prospects. Employees with opportunities for continuous learning are more engaged, motivated, and satisfied in their roles. This, in turn, leads to higher efficiency, increased employee retention, and a positive organizational culture.

To foster continuous learning, organizations can implement various strategies and initiatives. These may include establishing learning and development programs, providing access to online courses and educational resources, encouraging participation in conferences and industry events, and creating internal knowledge-sharing platforms. Regular performance evaluations and feedback sessions can also facilitate professional growth by identifying areas for improvement and setting development goals.

Continuous learning and improvement should be embraced at all levels of the organization, from individual contributors to leadership positions. Leaders play a vital part in creating a supportive learning environment by setting a positive example, promoting a growth mindset, and allocating resources for training and development initiatives. When continuous learning becomes an organizational priority, it becomes embedded in the organizational DNA, driving innovation and excellence.

VIII. Ensuring Compliance and Regulatory Requirements

A. Understanding compliance and regulatory considerations

In the DevSecOps ecosystem, understanding compliance and regulatory considerations is essential to ensure the development and delivery of secure and compliant software solutions. Compliance with industry regulations, privacy laws, and data protection standards is crucial for maintaining customer trust, avoiding legal repercussions, and safeguarding sensitive information.

DevSecOps, which integrates security practices into the software development process, provides an opportunity to address compliance requirements proactively. By considering compliance from the early stages of development, organizations can minimize the risk of non-compliance issues arising later in the software lifecycle.

One of the critical considerations is identifying and understanding the applicable regulatory frameworks and compliance standards that impact the organization's industry or geographical region. This includes FISMA, HIPAA, or PCI-DSS regulations. Familiarity with these standards helps organizations align their DevSecOps practices with the required controls and guidelines.

Mapping compliance requirements to specific DevSecOps practices is crucial. This involves identifying how security controls and processes align with regulatory obligations. For example, implementing secure coding practices, vulnerability scanning, and access controls can address data protection, confidentiality, and authentication requirements.

Documentation and evidence play a significant role in demonstrating compliance. Maintaining proper documentation of security controls, risk assessments, security testing results, and remediation efforts is vital. This documentation serves as evidence of compliance during audits or regulatory assessments.

Automation can significantly assist in achieving compliance in the DevSecOps ecosystem. By leveraging automation tools and practices, organizations can implement security controls consistently, perform vulnerability scans, conduct security testing, and enforce compliance checks throughout the software delivery pipeline. Automated compliance checks can detect and report any deviations from required configurations, ensuring adherence to regulatory guidelines.

Regular audits and assessments are essential for evaluating compliance within the DevSecOps ecosystem. Conducting internal audits, engaging external auditors, or performing self-assessments helps identify gaps in compliance and provides opportunities for remediation. These audits also enable organizations to monitor and improve their compliance posture continuously.

Collaboration and communication between development, security, and compliance teams are critical for successful compliance in DevSecOps. Encouraging cross-functional collaboration ensures that compliance requirements are understood and integrated into the development process. Regular meetings, shared documentation, and ongoing communication help maintain alignment and address compliance-related concerns.

Keeping pace with evolving compliance requirements is essential in the dynamic regulatory landscape. Organizations must stay informed about regulations, standards, and changes in industry best practices. Continuous monitoring of regulatory updates and active engagement with compliance forums or industry associations help ensure compliance practices remain current.

Table 17 **Demystifying FISMA:** Navigating Compliance and Security Standards

The Federal Information Security Management Act (FISMA) is a United States federal law enacted in 2002. It establishes a framework for protecting the information resources of federal agencies by requiring the implementation of security controls and risk management processes. FISMA aims to ensure the confidentiality, integrity, and availability of federal information and systems.

Controls	Description
Access Control:	Restricting access to authorized users and maintaining access logs.
Risk Assessment	Identifying and assessing risks to information and systems.
System and Communications Protection	Protecting the security and privacy of system communications and infrastructure.
Incident Response	Establishing procedures for detecting, responding to, and reporting security incidents.
Security Awareness and Training	Providing security awareness and training to personnel.
Configuration Management	Managing and controlling system configurations.
Contingency Planning	Developing plans for responding to and recovering from system disruptions or failures.
Identification and Authentication	Verifying the identity of users and devices accessing information systems.
Audit and Accountability	Generating and reviewing audit logs to ensure accountability and detect security breaches.
Security Assessment and Authorization	Conducting periodic assessments and authorizations of information systems to ensure compliance with security requirements.

Federal Information Security Management Act (FISMA) Assessment

Project Name *Enter Project Name*   Assessment Week *Select Week*

RAG	FISMA Assessment	Score Out of 5
	Risk Management Framework (RMF)	5
	Security Categorization	5
	Security Controls	5
	Security Assessment and Authorization (SA&A)	5
	Continuous Monitoring	5
	Incident Response	5

Risk Management Framework (RMF) radar chart and FISMA Assessment bar chart

Risk Management Framework (RMF)

The Federal Information Security Management Act (FISMA) Risk Management Framework (RMF) provides a structured and standardized process for managing security and privacy risks in federal information systems. The RMF consists of several parameters that guide the risk management process. Here are the key parameters of the FISMA RMF.

The Federal Information Security Management Act (FISMA) Risk Management Framework (RMF) provides a structured and standardized process for managing security and privacy risks in federal information systems. The RMF consists of several parameters that guide the risk management process. Below are the key parameters of the FISMA RMF. By assigning scores to each phase of the RMF process, you can monitor the progress and identify areas that require further attention or improvement. Regular assessment can be conducted to determine the current score for each phase, helping to track the overall effectiveness of the FISMA RMF implementation.

Start Self Assessment

Category	Description	Assessment	Score	Guidelines
Categorization	The first step in the RMF is to categorize the information system based on the potential impact of a security breach. This involves identifying the system's mission objectives, system components, data types, and potential impacts on the organization.		5	
Selection of Security Controls	Once the system is categorized, appropriate security controls are selected based on the impact level. areas are access control, identification and authentication, incident response, and configuration management.		5	
Implementation	In this phase, the selected security controls are implemented within the information system. This involves configuring hardware, software, and other security components, as well as documenting the implementation details.		5	
Assessment	The implemented security controls are then assessed to determine their effectiveness and compliance. This includes activities such as vulnerability scanning, penetration testing, and security control assessments. The assessment results are used to identify weaknesses and vulnerabilities in the system.		5	
Authorization	Based on the assessment results, an authorization decision is made to determine whether the system is acceptable for operation. This decision is made by the designated authorizing official (AO) who reviews the system's security posture, risk mitigation strategies, and residual risk.		5	
Continuous Monitoring	Once the system is authorized, continuous monitoring is conducted to ensure ongoing security. This includes real-time monitoring, incident detection and response, configuration management, and regular security status reporting.		5	
Remediation	If any security vulnerabilities or weaknesses are identified during the continuous monitoring process, appropriate actions are taken to mitigate the risks. This involves implementing patches, updates, and other corrective measures to address the identified issues.		5	
Reporting	Throughout the RMF process, documentation and reporting play a crucial role. Various reports are generated to capture the system's security status, risk assessment results, mitigation strategies, and other relevant information.		5	

Security Categorization

Security Categorization: FISMA mandates that federal agencies categorize their information systems based on the potential impact of a security breach. This categorization helps determine the appropriate level of security controls required.

The FISMA (Federal Information Security Management Act) Security Categorization is a process of evaluating the potential impact of a security breach on federal information systems. It helps determine the appropriate level of security controls required to protect the system. The security categorization is based on three key factors: confidentiality, integrity, and availability. Below are the FISMA security categorization levels. By assigning scores for each aspect of the security categorization, you can monitor and evaluate the effectiveness of the categorization process. Regular assessments and reviews can help identify areas that require improvement, provide feedback to stakeholders involved in the process, and ensure that the categorization accurately represents the potential impact of a security breach on the federal information system.

Start Self Assessment

Category	Description	Assessment	Score	Guidelines
Completeness	*To Be Added by Brother Sol Sravon*		5	**Low impact:** **Confidentiality:** The unauthorized disclosure of information would result in limited or no damage to the organization. **Integrity:** The unauthorized modification or destruction of information would have limited or no impact on the organization. **Availability:** The loss of information or system availability would have limited or no impact on the organization's ability to fulfill its mission.
Accuracy	*To Be Added by Brother Sol Sravon*		5	**Moderate impact:** **Confidentiality:** The unauthorized disclosure of information would have a serious adverse effect on the organization. **Integrity:** The unauthorized modification or destruction of information would have a serious adverse effect on the organization. **Availability:** The loss of information or system availability would have a serious adverse effect on the organization's ability to fulfill its mission.
Alignment with Organizational Requirements	*To Be Added by Brother Sol Sravon*		5	**High impact:** **Confidentiality:** The unauthorized disclosure of information would have a severe or catastrophic impact on the organization. **Integrity:** The unauthorized modification or destruction of information would have a severe or catastrophic impact on the organization. **Availability:** The loss of information or system availability would have a severe or catastrophic impact on the organization's ability to fulfill its mission. Management Framework.

Hands-on tool: Snapshot of FISMA

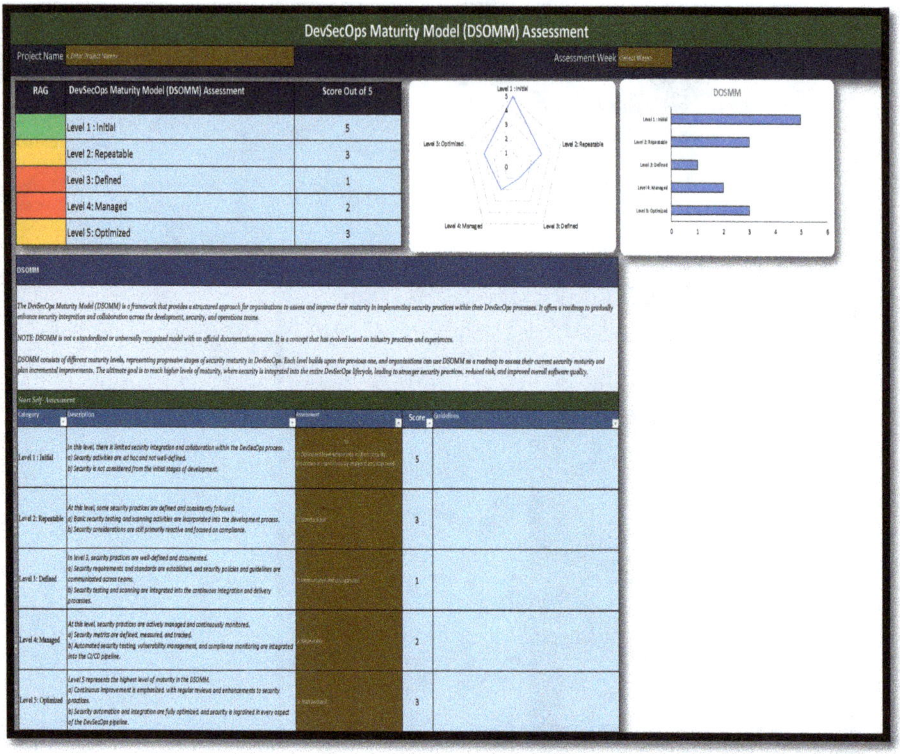

Hands-on tool: Snapshot of DSOMM

B. Incorporating security controls for compliance.

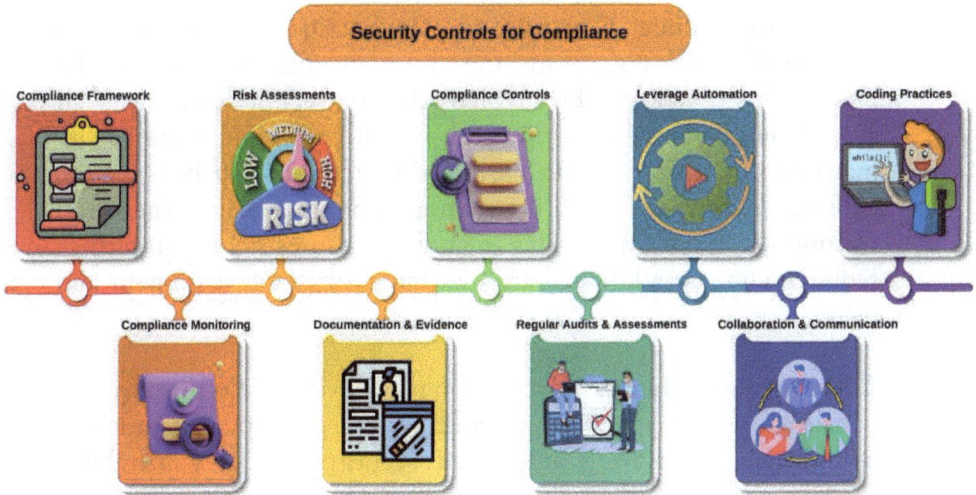

Incorporating security controls for compliance within the DevSecOps framework is crucial for organizations that build secure and compliant software solutions. By integrating compliance considerations into the development process, organizations can ensure that their applications adhere to industry regulations, privacy laws, and data protection standards. This section outlines key strategies for effectively incorporating security controls for compliance in the DevSecOps approach.

1. **Start with a Compliance Framework:** Identify the relevant compliance frameworks and regulations that apply to your organization, considering factors such as industry, geographic location, and the nature of data being handled. Standards like FISMA, HIPAA, and PCI-DSS are common examples. Understanding these frameworks helps shape the security controls required for compliance.

2. **Perform Risk Assessments:** Conducting comprehensive risk assessments enables organizations to identify potential security risks

and vulnerabilities associated with compliance. Organizations can prioritize security controls that align with compliance requirements by understanding the potential threats and impacts on data privacy and security.

3. **Map Compliance Controls to DevSecOps Practices:** Map compliance controls from the relevant frameworks to the DevSecOps practices. This involves aligning security controls, such as data encryption, access controls, audit trails, and vulnerability management, with specific DevSecOps activities, such as secure coding, automated testing, configuration management, and continuous monitoring. This mapping ensures that compliance requirements are addressed at every stage of the development and delivery process.

4. **Leverage Automation:** Automation plays a vital role in ensuring the consistent application of security controls and maintaining compliance. Employing automated security testing, vulnerability scanning, and configuration management tools streamlines the enforcement of security controls across the DevSecOps pipeline. Automation also helps maintain audit trails and generate necessary compliance reports efficiently.

5. **Secure Coding Practices:** Promote secure coding practices within the development teams. Encourage developers to follow secure coding guidelines, perform code reviews, and utilize static code analysis tools. By embedding security into the development process, companies can identify and rectify potential vulnerabilities early, ensuring compliance with security controls.

6. **Continuous Compliance Monitoring:** Implement continuous compliance monitoring to ensure adherence to security controls. Employ automated monitoring tools to detect deviations from compliance requirements in real time. Review and analyze logs, audit trails, and security events to promptly identify and address non-compliant activities.

7. **Documentation and Evidence:** Maintain comprehensive documentation and evidence of compliance efforts. Document security control implementations, risk assessments, vulnerability

remediation, and compliance testing results. This documentation is evidence during compliance audits and helps demonstrate a proactive approach to compliance requirements.

8. **Collaboration and Communication:** Facilitate collaboration and communication between development, security, and compliance teams. Encourage regular meetings, knowledge-sharing sessions, and cross-functional training. Promote a shared understanding of compliance objectives and foster a culture of collaboration to ensure all teams work towards a common goal of achieving compliance within the DevSecOps ecosystem.

9. **Regular Audits and Assessments:** Conduct regular assessments and audits to evaluate the effectiveness of security controls and ensure ongoing compliance. Perform internal audits or engage external auditors to validate compliance efforts and identify areas for improvement. Use audit findings to refine security controls and strengthen the compliance posture of the DevSecOps pipeline.

OSKAR Framework

To monitor and address security challenges in DevSecOps, one can leverage the Open Source Security Knowledge Au...

2.75 Overall Score

Security Automation
Security Testing
Security Monitoring
Security Metrics
Security Documentation

Security automation: Integrating security tools and scanners into the CI/CD pipeline | By integrating security tools and scanners into the CI/CD pipeline, the OSKAR framework ena... identify vulnerabilities and security issues early in the development process. This approach promotes a proactive security posture and streamlines security practices within the DevS... in the OSKAR framework, security automation refers to the process of integrating security tools and scanners into the CI/CD pipeline. This integration allows for automated security chec... lifecycle. Here are some details regarding security automation in the OSKAR framework & a simplified version of the scoring system for evaluating the implementation of security autom... format . Assign scores based on the level of implementation achieved for each criterion, with a range of 0 to 5, where 0 represents no implementation and 5 represents a fully implemented and mature state. Regularly reassess and update the scores to track progress and identify areas that require improvement.

Parameters	Measurement	Self-Assessment	Score	RAG Status
Tool Selection: Choose appropriate security tools and scanners that align with your organization's security requirements. These tools may include static code analysis (SAST) tools, dynamic application security testing (DAST) tools, software composition analysis (SCA) tools, container security scanners, and more.	**Tool Selection:** Appropriate security tool selection: Score based on the use of security tools that align with your organization's security requirements and cover a wide range of potential vulnerabilities and risks.	1: Unstructured and unorganized	1	
Integration in CI/CD Pipeline: Configure the security tools and scanners to be seamlessly integrated into your CI/CD pipeline. This integration ensures that security checks and tests are automatically triggered at the appropriate stages of the pipeline, such as during code builds, deployments, or before releases.	**Integration in CI/CD Pipeline:** Seamless integration in the pipeline: Score based on the successful integration of security tools and scanners into the CI/CD pipeline, ensuring that security checks and tests are automatically triggered at the appropriate stages.	2: Repeatable	2	
Static Application Security Testing (SAST): Incorporate SAST tools into the pipeline to analyze source code, identify potential security vulnerabilities, and enforce coding best practices. SAST scans can help detect issues like insecure coding patterns, hardcoded secrets, or common vulnerabilities.	**Static Application Security Testing (SAST):** Integration of SAST tools: Score based on the integration of SAST tools to analyze the source code, identify potential vulnerabilities, and enforce coding best practices.	3: Standardized	3	
Dynamic Application Security Testing (DAST): Integrate DAST tools to perform automated security testing by simulating real-world attacks against running applications. DAST scans can identify vulnerabilities exposed during runtime, such as injection attacks, cross-site scripting (XSS), or insecure configurations.	**Dynamic Application Security Testing (DAST):** Integration of DAST tools: Score based on the integration of DAST tools to perform automated security testing by simulating real-world attacks against running applications, identifying vulnerabilities exposed during runtime.	4: Managed and Monitored	4	
Software Composition Analysis (SCA): Use SCA tools to automatically scan and analyze third-party libraries and dependencies used in the codebase. These scans help identify known vulnerabilities or outdated versions of libraries that may introduce security risks.	**Software Composition Analysis (SCA):** Integration of SCA tools: Score based on the integration of SCA tools to scan and analyze third-party libraries and dependencies used in the codebase, identifying known vulnerabilities or outdated versions of libraries.	5: Optimized level, continuously analyzed and improved.	5	
Container Security Scanners: If your organization uses containerization technologies like Docker or Kubernetes, include container security scanners in the pipeline. These scanners examine container images for vulnerabilities, insecure configurations, and compliance violations, ensuring that containers are secure before deployment.	**Container Security Scanners:** Integration of container security scanners: Score based on the integration of container security scanners to examine container images for vulnerabilities, insecure configurations, and compliance violations before deployment.	1: Unstructured and unorganized	1	
Continuous Monitoring: Implement continuous monitoring solutions to track the security posture of your deployed applications and infrastructure. This can include tools for log monitoring, intrusion detection, security information and event management (SIEM), or cloud security monitoring, among others.	**Continuous Monitoring:** Implementation of continuous monitoring solutions: Score based on the implementation of continuous monitoring tools and processes to track the security posture of deployed applications and infrastructure, including log monitoring, intrusion detection, SIEM, or cloud security monitoring.	0: Not Implemented - Requirement Implementation Missing	0	
Automated Reporting and Alerting: Set up automated reporting and alerting mechanisms to provide timely notifications about security findings or vulnerabilities detected during the automated security checks. This enables prompt remediation and ensures that relevant stakeholders are informed.	**Automated Reporting and Alerting:** Implementation of automated reporting and alerting mechanisms: Score based on the implementation of automated reporting and alerting mechanisms to provide timely notifications about security findings or vulnerabilities detected during the automated security checks.	4: Managed and Monitored	4	

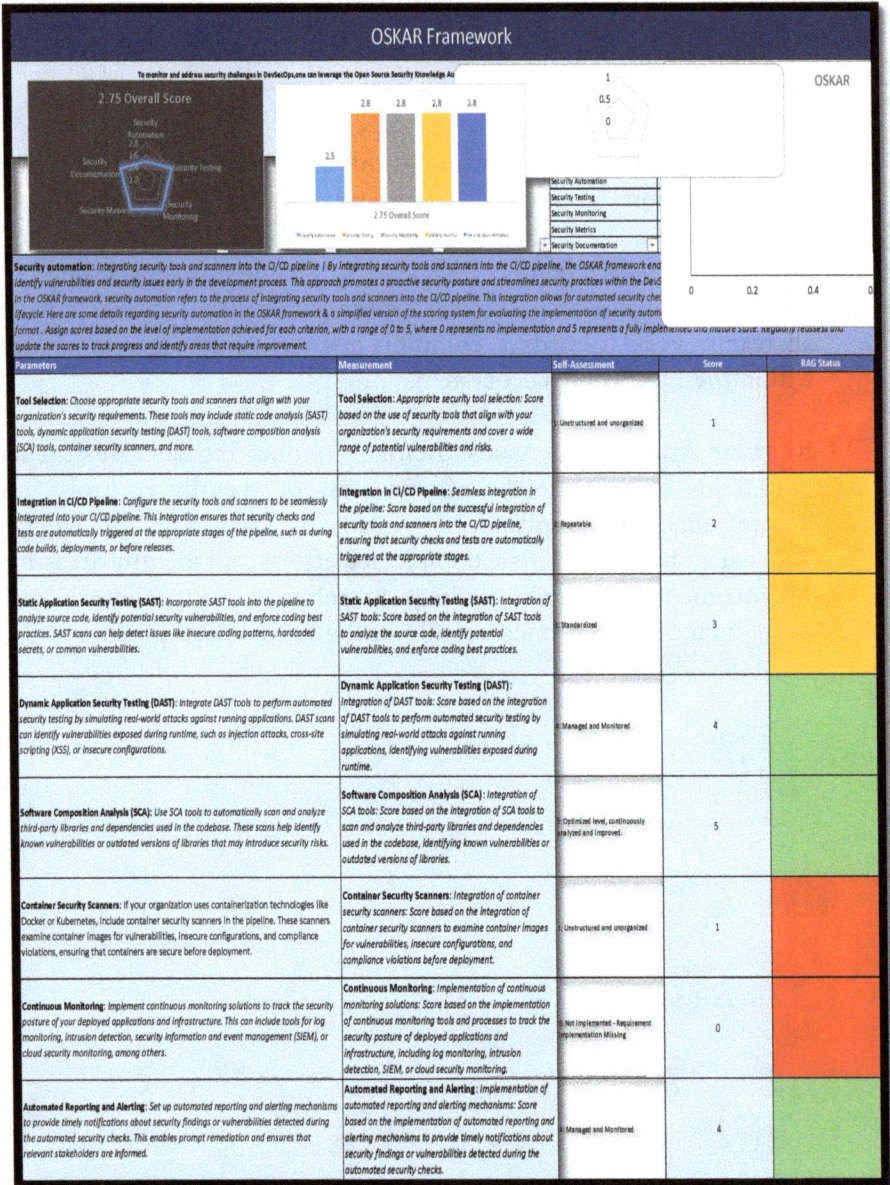

Hands-on tool: Snapshot of Open-Source Security Knowledge Automation (OSKAR) Framework.

C. Auditing and reporting for compliance.

Auditing and reporting for compliance within the DevSecOps ecosystem is essential for organizations prioritizing speed and Security in software development. By implementing robust auditing and reporting practices, organizations can demonstrate adherence to regulatory requirements, identify potential vulnerabilities, and ensure the integrity and Security of their software delivery pipeline. This article highlights the importance of auditing and reporting in the DevSecOps context and provides insights into best practices for effective compliance management.

1. **Define Compliance Requirements:** Begin by clearly defining the compliance requirements specific to your organization. Identify relevant regulations, industry standards, and internal policies that apply to your DevSecOps environment. These may include data protection regulations (e.g., GDPR, CCPA), industry-specific standards (e.g., PCI-DSS, HIPAA), or internal security policies. Understanding the compliance landscape helps shape your auditing and reporting framework.

2. **Integrate Security into the DevSecOps Pipeline:** DevSecOps emphasizes integrating security procedures into the software development process. Incorporate security controls and checkpoints throughout the DevSecOps pipeline, including secure coding practices, vulnerability assessments, security testing, and automated security scanning. Organizations can proactively address compliance requirements by integrating security measures during the development lifecycle.

3. **Implement Automated Security Auditing:** Automation is critical to efficient and effective auditing in the DevSecOps ecosystem. Utilize automated tools to conduct security audits, vulnerability scans, and configuration checks. Automated auditing enables organizations to identify security gaps, detect non-compliant activities, and monitor the effectiveness of security controls in real-time. Regularly scheduled audits and continuous monitoring provide an ongoing assessment of compliance status.

4. **Establish Log Monitoring and Event Management:** Implement log monitoring and event management systems to capture and analyze relevant security events and activities within the DevSecOps pipeline. Log aggregation and analysis tools help identify security incidents, track changes, and detect any anomalous behavior that may impact compliance. Robust event management capabilities enable prompt response and remediation actions.

5. **Regular Compliance Reporting:** Develop a systematic approach to compliance reporting, providing a clear and concise overview of compliance status to stakeholders. Regularly generate compliance reports highlighting adherence to specific regulations, industry standards, and internal policies. These reports should include details on security controls, vulnerabilities, remediation efforts, and any non-compliant activities. Transparent reporting helps demonstrate commitment to compliance and enables effective communication with auditors and regulatory bodies.

6. **Conduct Independent Audits and Assessments:** Engage independent auditors or conduct internal assessments to verify compliance adherence and identify areas for improvement. External audits objectively evaluate the DevSecOps ecosystem's compliance posture, ensuring alignment with regulatory requirements. Internal assessments help identify gaps or weaknesses in security controls and allow for timely remediation.

7. **Retain Audit Trail and Documentation:** Maintain a comprehensive audit trail and documentation that captures security events, changes, and compliance-related activities. Document all security controls, vulnerability assessments, incident response actions, and any modifications made to the DevSecOps environment. These records serve as evidence of compliance efforts and support future audits or investigations.

8. **Foster Collaboration and Communication:** Promote collaboration and communication between development, Security, and compliance teams. Establish channels for sharing audit findings, remediation plans, and security-related updates. Encourage cross-functional collaboration to align security requirements, compliance objectives, and development processes. Regular meetings, training

sessions, and knowledge-sharing activities foster a culture of collaboration and enhance compliance management efforts.

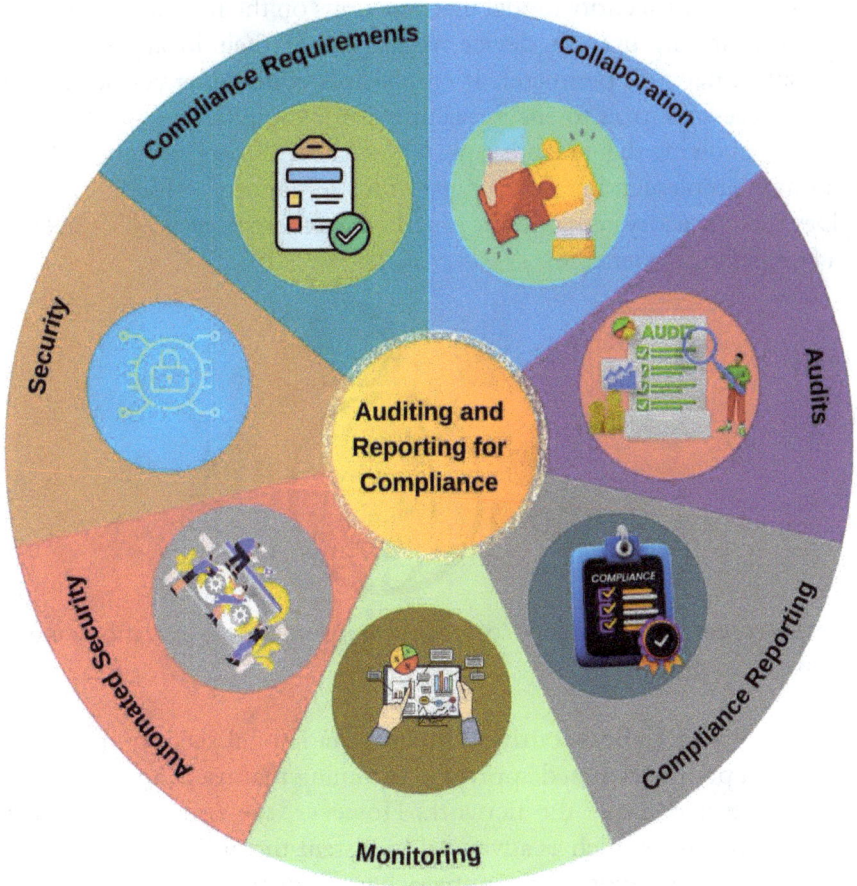

D. Protecting DevSecOps: Embracing a Zero Trust Approach

Zero Trust is a security model that functions on the hypothesis of having no trust in any user or device, regardless of their location within or outside a network perimeter. It emphasizes continuous verification and strict access controls to ensure security throughout the system. In today's rapidly evolving digital landscape, where cyber threats lurk around every corner, implementing the Zero Trust Maturity Model within a DevSecOps ecosystem goes beyond being a mere necessity—it becomes a compelling imperative.

Here are some reasons organizations may consider embracing the zero-trust model.

1. **Evolving Cybersecurity Threats**: Traditional security models rely on a perimeter-based approach, assuming that users and devices can be trusted inside the network. However, the rise of sophisticated cyber threats, such as advanced persistent threats (APTs) and insider threats, has rendered this approach inadequate. Zero Trust eliminates the assumption of Trust and treats every user, device, and network component as potentially compromised, ensuring that security measures are applied consistently throughout the ecosystem.

2. **Imagine an unsuspecting employee** inadvertently clicking on a malicious link in an email. In a zero-trust environment, even if the attacker gains access to the network, their lateral movement and access to sensitive data would be restricted, mitigating the breach's impact. Zero Trust's granular approach minimizes the attack surface and enables swift response and containment.

3. **Dynamic Workforce and Cloud Adoption**: The modern workforce is increasingly dynamic and distributed, with employees accessing resources from various devices, locations, and networks. Moreover, organizations are embracing cloud services and migrating critical workloads to hybrid or multi-cloud environments. This dynamic nature presents significant security challenges as traditional security models struggle to adapt to this new paradigm.

4. **Zero Trust** provides a unified security framework that extends beyond traditional network boundaries. It focuses on continuous authentication, authorization, and encryption, regardless of the user's location or the resources they are accessing. This approach ensures that security controls are context-aware, adaptive, and consistently applied across all environments, enabling secure access to resources irrespective of location.

5. **Regulatory Compliance and Data Privacy:** Compliance with regulatory standards like HIPAA and FISMA is paramount for organizations operating in various industries. Zero Trust can play a critical role in meeting these compliance requirements by enforcing strict access controls, auditing capabilities, and data protection measures.

Organizations can demonstrate a robust security posture by implementing a Zero Trust Maturity Model, ensuring that data privacy and regulatory obligations are effectively addressed. The model's principles of least privilege access, micro-segmentation, and continuous monitoring align with regulatory frameworks and empower organizations to achieve and maintain compliance more effectively.

The Zero Trust Maturity Model provides a compelling and convincing solution to the evolving cybersecurity landscape, the dynamic nature of modern workforces, and the imperative of regulatory compliance. By adopting this model within the DevSecOps ecosystem, organizations can enhance their security posture, safeguard critical assets, and effectively mitigate the risks posed by today's sophisticated cyber threats.

IX. Case Studies and Real-World Examples

A. Secure CI/CD Pipelines: Success Stories, Challenges, and Lessons Learned

DevSecOps combines development, security, and operations practices, and CI/CD (Continuous Integration/Continuous Delivery) pipelines have become integral components of modern software development. While they bring numerous benefits, they also present challenges that organizations must address. Here are some common challenges faced and lessons learned in DevSecOps and CI/CD pipeline implementations:

These examples demonstrate how organizations have applied the lessons learned in DevSecOps and CI/CD pipelines to enhance their software development practices.

	Challenge	Real-world Example	Lesson Learned
Security Integration	Incorporating security practices into the development process can be challenging. Security requirements and testing should seamlessly integrate into the CI/CD pipeline. It is essential to ensure that security scans, vulnerability assessments, and penetration testing are automated and included at appropriate pipeline stages.	Netflix's approach to security integration in their CI/CD pipeline is well-known. They have implemented a "Security Monkey" tool that continuously monitors their cloud infrastructure for security misconfigurations and alerts the development teams. This tool is integrated into their CI/CD pipeline, providing automated security checks and prioritizing security throughout development.	Insert security practices early in the development lifecycle, integrate security tools into the pipeline, and automate security checks.
Culture and Collaboration	Implementing DevSecOps and CI/CD requires a cultural shift and strong team collaboration. Developers, security experts, and operations personnel must collaborate closely, share responsibilities, and communicate effectively. Overcoming silos and fostering a culture of shared responsibility can be challenging.	Etsy, an e-commerce platform, emphasizes a strong culture of collaboration and shared responsibility. They have implemented a practice called "Blameless Post-Mortems," which encourages open communication and learning from failures. This approach fosters a culture of collaboration, where teams work together to address issues and share knowledge.	Foster a collaborative and cross-functional culture, encourage communication and knowledge sharing, and provide training to bridge team gaps.
Automated Testing	Effective testing is crucial in CI/CD pipelines, but organizations often struggle to maintain an adequate test suite and ensure proper coverage. Automating unit, integration, and end-to-end tests can be complex, especially when dealing with	Google has been a pioneer in automated testing. They employ a comprehensive testing framework called "Testing on the Toilet" (ToT). ToT provides bite-sized testing tips and best practices, ensuring that developers understand the importance of testing and have the necessary tools and knowledge to write practical tests.	Invest in building a comprehensive automated testing framework, prioritize test coverage, and leverage tools for test automation.

	diverse technologies and environments.		
Infrastructure as Code (IaC)	Managing infrastructure through code (IaC) is a crucial aspect of DevSecOps and CI/CD. Organizations face challenges in defining infrastructure requirements, managing configuration drift, and ensuring consistent deployments across different environments.	Airbnb utilizes IaC practices to manage its infrastructure. They have adopted Terraform as their IaC tool of choice. By defining their infrastructure as code, they can version control their infrastructure configurations, maintain consistency across environments, and automate deployments in a reliable and reproducible manner.	Adopt IaC practices using tools like Terraform or CloudFormation, version control infrastructure code, and implement automated deployment strategies.
Compliance and Governance	Organizations to adhere to various compliance standards and regulatory requirements. Ensuring compliance and maintaining governance within CI/CD pipelines can be complex, especially with the need for frequent releases and rapid iterations.	Capital One, a financial services company, has executed compliance checks within its CI/CD pipeline. They utilize a combination of automated security scans, vulnerability assessments, and compliance checks to ensure that their software meets regulatory requirements. This approach allows them to address compliance and governance concerns throughout the development lifecycle.	Implement compliance checks and controls within the pipeline, automate compliance checks, and document compliance processes.
Monitoring and Observability	Monitoring and observability become critical as CI/CD pipelines accelerate software delivery speed. Organizations must establish effective monitoring practices to identify and respond to real-time issues. Collecting and analyzing relevant metrics and logs can be	Slack, a communication and collaboration platform, emphasizes monitoring and observability in its CI/CD pipeline. They leverage tools like Prometheus and Grafana to collect and analyze metrics and logs. This enables them to gain insights into their application's performance, detect anomalies, and respond quickly to issues.	Implement robust monitoring and logging solutions, establish clear metrics and alerts, and invest in observability tools for real-time insights.

	challenging in dynamic environments.		
Continuous Learning and Improvement	The DevSecOps and CI/CD journey is ongoing. Organizations must continuously evaluate their pipeline, learn from failures, and adapt to changing requirements. Creating a philosophy of continuous improvement and learning from incidents is essential.	Amazon Web Services (AWS) employs a culture of continuous improvement in its DevSecOps practices. They conduct regular post-incident reviews (PIRs) to learn from incidents and identify areas for improvement. These PIRs help AWS refine its processes, update documentation, and enhance its CI/CD pipeline to prevent similar incidents in the future.	Encourage a learning culture, conduct post-incident reviews (PIRs), embrace feedback loops, and iterate on pipeline improvements.

While these challenges may seem daunting, addressing them can lead to more secure and efficient software development processes. Organizations should approach DevSecOps and CI/CD as iterative endeavors, constantly refining and optimizing their practices based on experience and industry best practices.

B. From Theory to Reality: Real-World Applications of IaC and PaC

Table 18 **From Theory to Reality:** Real-World Applications of IaC and PaC

The table below shows how Infrastructure as Code (IaC) and Policy as Code (PaC) are applied in various scenarios, making it easier to understand their practical applications and benefits along with real-world examples.

Infrastructure as Code (IaC)	Policy as Code (PaC)
Description	
An approach to managing and provisioning infrastructure using code files.	An approach to enforcing policies and compliance using code files.
Key Benefits	
- Consistency and Reproducibility - Version Control - Automated Provisioning - Documentation and Visibility - Scalability	- Consistency and Compliance - Automated Compliance Checking - Integration into CI/CD Pipelines - Audit Trail and Governance - Agility and Flexibility
Core Focus	
Managing infrastructure configurations as Code.	Defining policies and security controls as Code.
Tools	
Terraform, CloudFormation, Ansible, Puppet, Chef, etc.	Custom scripts, Regula, Open Policy Agent (OPA), Conftest, etc.
Implementation	
- Infrastructure setup using machine-readable definition files. - Versioning and tracking changes in version control systems. - Automated provisioning and configuration management. - Increased scalability and environment consistency. - Infrastructure orchestration for multi-tier applications.	- Policies are defined in the Code with specific criteria and rules. - Automated checks for policy compliance. - Integration into CI/CD pipelines for continuous monitoring. - Maintain an audit trail of policy checks and enforcement. - Policy-as-code used for security, governance, and compliance.
Use Cases	

- Provisioning cloud resources (VMs, databases, storage) in AWS/Azure/GCP. - Automating server configuration (installing software, setting up networks). - Scaling applications based on demand with auto-scaling groups. - Replicating staging environments to production.	- Enforcing security policies related to access controls. - Ensuring compliance with industry standards (HIPAA, GDPR). - Enforcing configuration standards across cloud resources. - Automating compliance checks in CI/CD pipelines.
Real-world Example	
- Using Terraform to provision AWS EC2 instances and set up load balancers. - Using Ansible to automate software installation and configuration on servers. - Configuring networking and security groups through AWS CloudFormation. - Replicating Kubernetes namespaces and resources from one cluster to another.	- Implementing PaC with Open Policy Agent (OPA) to enforce Kubernetes cluster security. - Using Conftest to ensure container images adhere to compliance. - Creating custom policies to enforce specific corporate guidelines. - Enforcing role-based access controls (RBAC) for cloud resources.

X. Conclusion

In the contemporary landscape of software development, securing the CI/CD pipeline is an undertaking of paramount significance. Within this crucible, organizations face the challenge of preserving the integrity and resilience of their software delivery processes. By embracing the tenets of DevSecOps, implementing best practices, harnessing the power of automation and tooling, and nurturing a culture of collaboration between development and security teams, organizations can raise the vanguard of security for their CI/CD pipelines. Continuous monitoring, the regular crucible of security testing, and a proactive stance on security issues equip organizations to unearth and mitigate vulnerabilities in their nascent stages, resulting in a software delivery process that is both more resilient and more secure.

A Dynamic Security Landscape:

As technology evolves and threats continue to evolve and increase, organizations must adapt their security practices to keep pace with the ever-changing risks. By giving paramount importance to pipeline security and unwaveringly adhering to the best practices delineated in this white paper, organizations erect a robust DevSecOps framework. This framework is not merely a line of defense; it is a citadel of protection, assuring the security and integrity of their CI/CD pipelines. In so doing, organizations stand as vigilant sentinels, safeguarding their applications and the sanctity of sensitive data.

The path to securing the CI/CD pipeline is not a solitary journey; it is a collective endeavor. It is a journey characterized by vigilance, innovation, collaboration, and an unwavering commitment to security. The imperative for a more secure and resilient software delivery process transcends the confines of choice; it is a strategic mandate.

A. Recap of key points discussed.

A recap of the critical aspects discussed regarding securing the CI/CD pipeline and adopting DevSecOps practices.

The CI/CD pipeline plays a crucial role in software development, automating the process of building, testing, and deploying software changes. However, security concerns have emerged as CI/CD pipelines become popular. Attackers target pipelines due to their automated and rapid nature, leading to potential vulnerabilities and risks.

To address these concerns, organizations are adopting DevSecOps, which integrates security practices into the CI/CD pipeline from the early stages of development. DevSecOps emphasizes collaboration, automation, and shared responsibility for security among development, operations, and security teams.

Understanding the CI/CD pipeline involves recognizing its components, phases, and stages while acknowledging the security challenges faced at each phase. These challenges include insecure coding practices, compromised build servers, inadequate security testing, and vulnerabilities during deployment.

Implementing DevSecOps practices offers numerous benefits, including early detection of vulnerabilities, reduced security breaches, improved incident response, and enhanced compliance. DevSecOps principles revolve around shifting security left, automating security processes, integrating security testing, and fostering a security-aware culture.

Best practices for safeguarding the CI/CD pipeline encompass threat modeling, secure coding practices, continuous vulnerability scanning, securing the build and deployment processes, access controls, monitoring and logging, security testing, and secure configuration management.

Automation and tooling are vital for pipeline security. Security tools and technologies, such as SAST, DAST, SCA, and container security, can be integrated into the pipeline. Automation facilitates security policy enforcement and improves efficiency in identifying and addressing security issues.

Securing containerized environments requires best practices like using trusted images, updating containers and components, applying least privilege, network segmentation, and vulnerability scanning. Secure utilization of container orchestration platforms, such as Kubernetes, includes securing the control plane, access control, encryption, and auditing.

Collaboration between development and security teams is critical. Educating developers on secure coding practices and establishing security champions within development teams foster a security-aware culture and effective collaboration.

Ensuring compliance and regulatory requirements involves incorporating security controls, conducting audits, and generating compliance reports aligned with industry-specific standards and regulations.

Real-world case studies highlight successful implementations of secure CI/CD pipelines, challenges faced, and lessons learned, providing practical insights and inspiration.

In conclusion, securing the CI/CD pipeline is critical to protect software development processes. Adopting DevSecOps practices, integrating security at every stage, leveraging automation and tooling, securing containerized environments, fostering collaboration, and ensuring compliance can enhance pipeline security and deliver secure software efficiently.

B. Emphasizing the importance of securing the CI/CD pipeline.

Securing the CI/CD pipeline is paramount in today's software development landscape. As organizations strive for faster software updates and feature delivery, the pipeline becomes a prime target for attackers. Neglecting pipeline security can lead to compromised software, data breaches, and significant financial and reputational damage. By adopting DevSecOps practices and integrating security into every pipeline phase, organizations can proactively identify and mitigate vulnerabilities, minimize security risks, and ensure secure software delivery. Robust pipeline security enhances the organization's ability to respond to security incidents, meets compliance and regulatory requirements, and fosters a culture of security awareness among development and operations teams. Securing the CI/CD pipeline safeguards software development processes and protects valuable assets.

C. Harnessing DevSecOps for Uncompromising Pipeline Security

Securing the CI/CD pipeline is paramount for organizations aiming to protect their software development processes and valuable assets. By adopting DevSecOps practices, organizations can bolster their pipeline's security posture, proactively mitigating vulnerabilities and staying ahead of evolving threats.

DevSecOps encapsulates a transformative approach integrating security throughout the CI/CD pipeline. This collaborative paradigm emphasizes shared responsibility, automation, and a culture of security awareness among development, operations, and security teams. With DevSecOps, security becomes an intrinsic element from the early stages of development, ensuring the detection and remediation of vulnerabilities before they jeopardize software integrity.

Implementing DevSecOps practices yields a host of benefits. Organizations can detect vulnerabilities at their nascent stages, reducing the risk of security disruptions and data leaks. Swift incident response capabilities bolster resilience, minimizing the impact of potential threats. Furthermore, embracing DevSecOps fosters a security-centric culture, empowering developers to implement secure coding practices and utilize automation and tooling to fortify their codebase.

DevSecOps provides a proactive defense against compliance and regulatory requirements. By adhering to industry standards and integrating security controls, organizations can demonstrate their commitment to safeguarding sensitive data and meeting legal obligations. Moreover, organizations can safeguard their reputation and build trust among users, investors, and stakeholders by adopting DevSecOps practices.

In conclusion, adopting DevSecOps practices is imperative for organizations seeking robust pipeline security. By integrating security throughout the CI/CD pipeline, organizations can detect vulnerabilities early, enhance incident response, and foster a culture of security awareness. Embracing DevSecOps enables organizations to comply with regulations, protect valuable assets, and demonstrate their unwavering commitment to security.

XI. Open-Source Tool

Comprehensive Guide to Using DevSecOps CI/CD Pipeline Open-Source Project Monitoring, Self-Assessment, and Metric Management Tool:

Integrating security into the DevOps pipeline, known as DevSecOps, has become a crucial practice. To empower organizations to achieve this balance between speed and security, open-source tools are available to monitor projects, conduct self-assessments, and manage technical and project metrics effectively. This guide will delve into each category to equip you with a comprehensive understanding of using these tools proficiently.

Project Monitoring Tool
1. DevSecOps Project Monitoring Tool
DevSecOps Project Monitoring Tools provide real-time insights into the security posture of applications throughout their lifecycle. These tools seamlessly integrate security into the DevOps process, ensuring robust protection.

Key Features:

- Real-time Security Insights

- Integration with CI/CD Pipelines

- Vulnerability Scanning

- Continuous Monitoring

How to Use:

1. Integrate the chosen monitoring tool into your CI/CD pipeline.

2. Configure the tool to scan code repositories and containers.

3. Set up alerts for security vulnerabilities.

4. Continuously monitor the tool's dashboard for insights.

5. Remediate identified vulnerabilities promptly.

6. Use the tool's reporting capabilities to track security improvements over time.

Self-Assessment Tool

2. Assessment of Security Challenges with DevSecOps

This tool assesses and mitigates unique security risks and obstacles in DevSecOps adoption, helping organizations balance speed and security effectively.

Key Features:

- Security Risk Assessment

- Mitigation Strategies

- Best Practice Guidance

How to Use:

1. Conduct an initial assessment of your organization's DevSecOps practices.

2. Identify security challenges and vulnerabilities.

3. Develop mitigation strategies and action plans.

4. Implement security best practices.

5. Regularly review and update the assessment to track progress.

3. Infrastructure as Code (IaC) Best Practices Assessment

This tool evaluates how infrastructure is defined and provisioned using code, optimizing efficiency, reliability, and security in modern cloud environments.

Key Features:

- IaC Code Review

- Security Scanning

- Compliance Checks

How to Use:

1. Analyze your IaC codebase for security and compliance issues.

2. Implement security scanning and compliance checks into your CI/CD pipeline.

3. Automate code reviews and remediate issues.

4. Continuously monitor IaC for security and compliance.

4. Policy as Code (PaC) Best Practice Assessment

This tool defines and enforces security and compliance policies through code, ensuring adherence to specified standards.

Key Features:

- Policy Definition

- Code Enforcement

- Compliance Reporting

How to Use:

1. Define security and compliance policies as code.

2. Implement policy enforcement mechanisms.

3. Continuously monitor and enforce policies.

4. Generate compliance reports for auditing purposes.

5. Fortify and Flourish: Mastering Container Security and Self-Assessment

Container security is vital in DevSecOps. This tool helps master container security practices and conduct self-assessments for secure containerized applications.

Key Features:

- Container Scanning

- Image Vulnerability Assessment

- Container Runtime Security

How to Use:

1. Integrate container scanning and vulnerability assessment into your CI/CD pipeline.

2. Continuously scan container images for vulnerabilities.

3. Implement runtime security measures.

4. Conduct periodic self-assessments to ensure container security.

6. Technical Debt Assessment in DevSecOps

Managing technical debt involves evaluating and addressing suboptimal practices in software development. This tool helps maintain a sustainable security posture.

Key Features:

- Technical Debt Analysis

- Remediation Planning

- Code Quality Metrics

How to Use:

1. Analyze code repositories for technical debt.

2. Prioritize and plan remediation efforts.

3. Implement code quality metrics in CI/CD.

4. Monitor and reduce technical debt over time.

7. Zero Trust Maturity Model

The Zero Trust Maturity Model outlines a framework for progressively adopting a Zero Trust security approach. It enhances security by continuously verifying trustworthiness.

Key Features:

- Zero Trust Assessment

- Trust Verification
- Security Enhancements

How to Use:

1. Assess your organization's current security posture.

2. Implement Zero Trust principles and verification mechanisms.

3. Continuously monitor trust levels and enhance security measures.

8. Federal Information Security Management Act (FISMA) Assessment

This assessment evaluates and ensures compliance with federal information security standards and regulations, crucial for government agencies and sensitive data handling.

Key Features:

- FISMA Compliance Check
- Security Controls Assessment
- Documentation Auditing

How to Use:

1. Identify applicable FISMA requirements.

2. Conduct a comprehensive compliance assessment.

3. Implement necessary security controls and documentation.

4. Regularly audit and update compliance records.

9. DevSecOps Maturity Model (DSOMM) Assessment

The DSOMM Assessment helps organizations gauge their maturity in integrating security into the DevOps pipeline, guiding them toward continuous improvement.

Key Features:

- Maturity Assessment

- Best Practice Adoption

- Improvement Roadmap

How to Use:

1. Evaluate your DevSecOps practices against DSOMM benchmarks.

2. Identify areas for improvement.

3. Adopt best practices and integrate security into your pipeline.

4. Follow the DSOMM roadmap for maturity growth.

10. Open-Source Security Knowledge Automation (OSKAR) Framework

The OSKAR Framework automates the acquisition and application of open-source security knowledge, systematically enhancing your organization's security posture.

Key Features:

- Knowledge Acquisition

- Automation Rules

- Knowledge Application

How to Use:

1. Define security knowledge acquisition sources.

2. Create automation rules for knowledge application.

3. Implement automation within your CI/CD pipeline.

4. Continuously update knowledge sources and regulations.

Metric Management Tool
11. Technical and Project Metric Management Tools
Metric Definitions

Clarify key performance indicators (KPIs) and metrics used to measure the effectiveness and efficiency of DevSecOps practices.

Key Features:

- KPI Identification

- Metric Definition

- Data Collection Methods

How to Use:

1. Identify KPIs relevant to your DevSecOps objectives.

2. Define metrics and measurement methods.

3. Establish data collection processes.

4. Continuously review and refine metrics.

12. Sample DevSecOps Technical Dashboard

A Sample DevSecOps Technical Dashboard visually represents essential security and operational metrics, helping teams monitor and manage DevSecOps processes effectively.

Key Features:

- Visual Data Representation

- Customizable Dashboards

- Real-time Updates

How to Use:

1. Customize the dashboard to display relevant metrics.

2. Integrate data sources and update frequency.

3. Share the dashboard with relevant stakeholders.

4. Analyze data to make informed decisions.

13. Data

Data is the foundation of any DevSecOps initiative. Discuss data collection, storage, analysis, and visualization techniques critical for decision-making in DevSecOps practices.

Key Features:

- Data Collection Strategies

- Data Storage Solutions

- Data Analysis Tools

How to Use:

1. Determine data sources, including logs, metrics, and security events.

2. Implement data collection mechanisms.

3. Choose appropriate data storage solutions.

4. Utilize data analysis tools to extract insights.

5. Visualize data

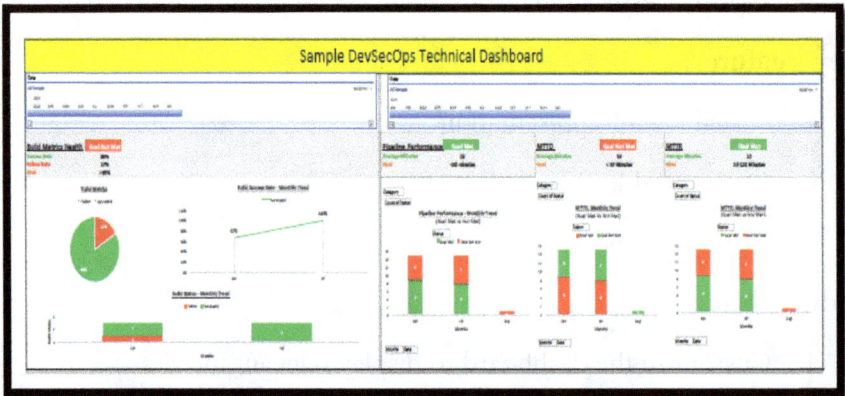

Sample DevSecOps Technical Dashboard

XII. References

1) **Netflix Tech Blog:**
https://lnkd.in/dFpm7Xxz

2) **Netflix Open Source:**
https://netflix.github.io/

3) **Netflix Architecture:**
https://lnkd.in/dUmxWhNd

4) **Etsy:**
https://www.etsy.com/codeascraft/quantum-of-deployment/

https://www.etsy.com/codeascraft

5) **Google:**
https://cloud.google.com/customers/etsy

https://testing.googleblog.com/

https://testing.googleblog.com/2013/05/testing-on-toilet-dont-overuse-mocks.html

6) **Airbnb:**
https://medium.com/airbnb-engineering/continuous-delivery-at-airbnb-6ac042bc7876

https://aws.amazon.com/solutions/case-studies/airbnb-expanding-online-marketplace-case-study/

7) **CapitalOne:**
https://www.capitalone.com/tech/software-engineering/realigning-devops-practices-to-support-microservices/

8) **Slack:**
https://slack.com/blog/collaboration/real-time-collaboration-tools-you-should-integrate-into-slack#:~:text=Top%20online%20collaboration%20tools%20for%20meetings,-With%20remote%20meetings&text=We're%20partial%20to%20Slack,project%20conversations%20and%20issues%20simultaneously.

About the Author:

With over two decades of distinguished experience, I am a skilled and proficient professional currently serving as a DevSecOps Technical Advisor and Program Manager. My expertise spans IT project management, meticulous acquisition package preparation, precise cost estimation, innovative systems design, seamless data migration, information security management, comprehensive risk assessment, and a dedicated commitment to regulatory compliance.

My track record demonstrates a consistent ability to orchestrate flawless project execution, allocate resources prudently, and precisely oversee capital planning and investment control. I have successfully navigated multiple program portfolios, implementing robust controls to proactively identify and mitigate information-related risks.

My relentless pursuit of excellence, attention to detail, and dedication to IT governance principles position me as a catalyst for success in Program Management, Systems Engineering, and Project Engineering. As a DevSecOps Technical Advisor and Program Manager, I showcase exceptional mastery in DevSecOps, IT operations, compliance, and project management. I have successfully constructed CI/CD pipelines and crafted DevSecOps dashboards, ensuring seamless operation and impervious security of IT processes.

My leadership extends to managing program portfolios, delivering dynamic technical presentations, and spearheading complex data migration initiatives. I excel in designing, developing, and managing robust security systems in IT security and compliance, adhering unwaveringly to the federal government and IT regulatory standards.

I actively contribute to IT capital planning and investment control processes, aligning technology investments with organizational objectives. My strategic insight is evident in addressing intricate software challenges by implementing a comprehensive Root Cause Analysis (RCA) framework.

Furthermore, my career is characterized by unwavering devotion to excellence, technical acumen, and successful implementation of pivotal frameworks. Active participation in compliance audits underscores my commitment to upholding the highest quality and regulatory standards. With a rich tapestry of skills and extensive experience, I consistently serve as an invincible force for success in critical domains, including Program Management, Systems Engineering, and Project Engineering.

www.ingramcontent.com/pod-product-compliance
Lightning Source LLC
Chambersburg PA
CBHW050451190326
41458CB00005B/1236